I0470324

Job Strategies for the 21st Century: How to Assist Today's College Students during Economic Turbulence

"Students in today's economic fallout are feeling tremendous apprehension regarding their future in the real world. Dr. Green and Mr. Bailey provide wonderful insights in assisting students to make intelligent, informed, and strategic decisions beyond the classroom."

- BRANDI REILLY,

**PROJECT MANAGER FOR SHAW
ENVIRONMENTAL & INFRASTRUCTURE**

"Dr. Green and Mr. Bailey do an excellent job of explaining how to build a life rather than just getting a job. If you are going to spend 40+ hours a week at an income-earning activity you might as well select and attain a position that fits you and for which you enjoy 'going to work' everyday. This book is a must-read for anyone who is thinking of starting a new profession or re-evaluating what he/she is currently doing."

- BRUCE E. WINSTON, PHD

**DEAN
REGENT UNIVERSITY
SCHOOL OF GLOBAL LEADERSHIP &
ENTREPRENEURSHIP**

"Tough economic times demand new strategies to win employment with today's employment market place awash in highly qualified and highly motivated candidates....This book should be on every community college, college, and university academic adviser and career service adviser's desk."

DR PAUL HOFFMAN, DSL

**ADJUNCT PROFESSOR, BELLEVUE
UNIVERSITY, COLLEGE OF ARTS
AND SCIENCES, CENTER FOR
COMMUNICATION ARTS.**

"Dr. Green and Mr. Bailey changed my idea in how to look for a job in these uncertain economic times. This book should be read by anybody who really wants to increase the chances to land a new job."

JOSE VASQUEZ,

**APPLIED RESEARCH CENTER
RESEARCHER**

"Job Strategies for the 21st Century provides practical as well as inspiring insights for anyone planning on competitively advancing themself in a challenging job market. A must-read for current students and job seekers."

RYAN ZEKRY,

NEW AMSTERDAM BAR & GRILL OWNER / MBA STUDENT

"Authors Green and Bailey have taken a realistic and motivating heartfelt approach to one of the most anxiety-generating topics on the minds of today's college students and recent graduates – the impending 'World of Work.'"

LARRY D. THACKER,

M.ED., LINCOLN MEMORIAL UNIVERSITY, DIRECTOR OF STUDENT SUCCESS, RETENTION, AND CAREER SERVICES. AUTHOR OF *MOUNTAIN MYSTERIES: THE MYSTIC TRADITIONS OF APPALACHIA*

"What can I say... the authors' thoroughness in detailing this book proves how interested they are in the success of today's college students. If you need an elaborate and systematic plan of action, read this book."

LESLIE HAMLETT,

MS, INSTRUCTIONAL TECHNOLOGY TENNESSEE EARLY CHILDHOOD TRAINING ALLIANCE, PROFESSIONAL DEVELOPMENT TRAINER/SPECIALIST

"Dr. Green gives the reader a clear and concise road map infused with practical ideas that should help any soon to be graduate or one-to-two year post graduate understand the job market and what it takes to market their skills for success. I wish such a book was available when I began my job search right out of college. It wouldn't have taken me years to obtain the perfect job for me!"

DR. DESHAUN H. DAVIS,

**PROFESSOR, ECONOMIST, CONSULTANT
NORTHERN VIRGINIA COMMUNITY
COLLEGE
ANNANDALE, VIRGINIA**

"What an awesome book and learning tool for managers and leaders to have in their possession. Very insightful information."

TRACY H. WHITAKER

AUTHOR & EDUCATOR

"While the focus of Job Strategies for the 21st Century is to provide valuable assistance to graduating college students in formulating job strategies, it is a good read and can be an invaluable tool for individuals of all ages. It contains a little of a lot, including, statistics, advice, great quotes and good old common sense. I commend its message to anyone who is seeking success in a job market struggling to recover from our most recent recession of 2009."

BARBARALETTE G. DAVIS

**ASSISTANT CITY ATTORNEY
CITY OF MEMPHIS**

All Rights Reserved. Copyright © 2011 by PMLA Press 2nd edition

All rights reserved. Except as permitted under the Copyright Act of 1976, no part of this publication may be reproduced or distributed in any form or by any means, electronic or mechanical, including photocopying and recording, or stored on any information storage or retrieval system, without the written permission of the publisher.

Although the authors and publisher have exhaustively researched all sources to ensure the accuracy and completeness of the information contained in this book, we assume no responsibility for errors, inaccuracies, omissions, or any inconsistency herein. Anything appearing derogatory to people or organizations is unintentional. Readers should use their own judgment or an attorney or other experts for their individual concerns.

Graphic images are credited to
iStock (www.istockphoto.com) and Microsoft (www.microsoft.com).
Graphic Designer: Catalin S. (www.vektorial.ro)

For information on ordering in bulk, please contact:

PMLA
P.O. Box 32733
Knoxville, TN 37930-2733
(865) 602-7858
advice@darylgreen.org
www.darylgreen.org

I press toward the mark for the prize of the high calling of God in Christ Jesus.

- PHILIPPIANS 3:14

· · · · · · · · · · · · · ·

· · · · · · · · · · · · · ·

Dedication

This book is dedicated to the millions of college students trying to survive in these uncertain times.

Table of Contents

Preface

Dr. Daryl D. Green

People are losing their jobs. Retirees are losing their retirements. US companies are losing market share due to competition abroad. Is there any wonder why college students are losing hope in finding a good job for the future? I have been to many campuses and seen that many students are not prepared for the hectic competition for today's jobs. This project was developed as a result of my experiences during my time as a visiting professor with the National Urban League's Black Executive Exchange Program. As I visited Lane College and Winston-Salem State University, I was deeply moved by the students and wanted to do more to assist all students in transitioning to full employment. Sadly, it was clear to me that many of the past approaches for college students did not consider the current economic troubles. Therefore, many students are being left in a very bad situation. For example, they must now compete with more seasoned individuals for an entry level job. I hope to challenge students to think about a personal job strategy for securing the right job. I could not have found a better partner than William "Bill" Bailey. Bill and I have participated in a number of projects together that address the needs of young people. I believe that God has a special purpose for each of us. Therefore, it is important to provide students new strategies in order to deal with future uncertainties in the job market.

William Bailey

We are all born with special talents, gifts, and interests. Within every difficulty, or even crisis in life, there lies an opportunity. Amazingly, those who rise to the challenges of our day are deemed leaders. From our youth, we prepared to become future leaders, in some small or large way, and our success is a result of our will to determine our legacy. For contemporary college-aged adults, the future is now, and the challenge is ultimately to pursue our divinely appointed passions, even in a seriously troubled economic world. I am passionate about addressing the needs of these future students and equipping them with the necessary tools and practical knowledge to be successful. Having been there, as a despondent college graduate, and by engaging today's students as guest lecturers, we know and understand the importance for students to plan for their career goals. Daryl and I believe most college students neglect the need for career planning. It is either due to a lack of knowledge, hope, or both. I have worked with Daryl for several years, and it is his passion to see others purse and achieve their God-given purpose in life. It is our desire that this book will change your perspective, and be a source of information, encouragement, and hope.

Job Strategies for the 21st Century provides practical solutions to the challenges that today's college students need when attempting to find employment in an unstable economy. This book is also designed for parents of college students, college recruiters, career centers, employers, libraries, and other supporters of young people. This book is brief and concise and can be easily disseminated across all social networks (e.g. Facebook and MySpace, etc.), and can be a guide to many struggling graduates who are considering giving up. As adults, we must mentor our young people and help them discover what truly makes them special to discover what it is that truly makes them special. With a new sense of direction, we hope that today's college students and graduates will be encouraged to pursue their real dreams, regardless of life's circumstances.

Acknowledgement

We wish to take this opportunity first to thank God for guiding our footsteps and giving His son, Jesus, to our world. We humbly want to thank our immediate families—our wives and our children. Lord, you continue to supply us with your abundant love. You know we all need loving and supportive people to produce a special project that will be a blessing to others. Thank you for sending special people into our lives who supported us that we too may be a blessing! We want to thank everyone who read, evaluated, and commented on our book. We want to especially thank Dr. Dahlia Cunningham for her support in this book development. Your critical contributions and feedback helped make this book a reality.

Finally, we want to thank our many friends who gave us tremendous support. There are too many to mention. We understand this accomplishment was not achieved solely on our own merit. May God continue to bless your life's journey with Him.

Introduction

Wendy was a model college student. She felt that her grades were good enough to land her a good paying job. She was wrong! Despite being at the top of her class, she found herself frustrated, unemployed, and competing with a million or more experienced workers. When she finally landed a job, it did not even require a degree! Later after settling in on the job, she considered her present situation, and wondered, "Was all this college stuff just a waste of time?"

So, the question is, are you prepared to land a job in today's difficult job market? If not, you're not alone. The make-up of graduating students today is a hodgepodge of traditional and non-traditional students, which raises the level of competition. According to a report filed by the National Center for Education Statistics (2000), a 'traditional' (undergraduate) student is defined as a full-time enrollee at a postsecondary institution (for less-than-2-years, 2-years, or 4-years), who enrolled immediately after earning a high school diploma. These full-time enrollees are typified by being completely financially dependent on parents or guardians for financial support, and are not gainfully employed throughout the school year[1]. Conversely, according to this same report, a 'non-traditional' student is more broadly defined as one whose enrollment is delayed for more than a year after earning a high school diploma/GED (if at all), attending as a part-time enrollee, working full-time while enrolled, and are financially independent with regard to qualifying for sponsored financial aid.

The U.S. Department of Education estimates that 90 million individuals participate in some form of adult education each year. This includes training and basic education offered outside traditional academia. To address this emerging market, many colleges have developed programs and services geared toward adult learners. According to the Department of Education, 40% of American college students (almost 6 million people) are 25 years of age or older.[2] As of March 2010, the Bureau of Labor Statistics website

---

1   *"Findings from the Condition of Education 2002," by Susan Choy*
2   *"Federal Student Aid," by U.S. Department of Education*

reported that there were roughly 15 million people unemployed, resulting in an unemployment rate of 9.7%.[3] Simply put, landing a job today is an extreme uphill challenge, considering the large number of graduating students combined with the rising number of the unemployed. Currently, college graduates find themselves competing with other individuals who are more seasoned and experienced for basic entry level positions in their career field.

As the financial crisis continues, and with the US labor market severely weakening, many college students are wondering how they will survive these difficult times. Businesses operate in retreat instead of expansion. Other government reports indicate that temporary jobs jumped in February 2010 to two million which was up 284,000 since September 2009.[4] With such fierce competition today for limited jobs, understandably many wonder if they will be able to land 'a good job' in the marketplace, while others grow weary with the continuous stress of making ends meet.[5] In fact, CareerCast. com analyzed 21 different factors that contribute to job stress for those who are employed and ranked over 200 professions that were the most stressful (see Table 1), some of whom are also seeking different employment.[6] Obviously there is a lot of frustration out there. The mistake is that many employed persons continue to believe that their company will take a vested interest in their career development. This is simply not true. Rarely will an employee retire from their initial place of employment. However, today's job market demands that college students develop their own personal strategy for employment. From our experience, acting as student advocates in academic and community settings, we frequently find ourselves encouraging students to plan for their career aspirations. This book provides some traditional and less traditional steps for effectively positioning current college students to better compete in future job markets.

---

3   *Bureau of Labor Statistics website*
4   *Bureau of Labor Statistics website*
5   *"How to overcome burnout from a dead end job," by Daryl D. Green*
6   *CNBC.com. "America's most stressful jobs in 2010," by CNBC.com*

Job Strategies for the 21st Century provides today's college students and graduates with innovative strategies for positioning themselves in a tough economic market where jobs are very limited, and the economy is unstable. The book is designed for recent graduates as well as nontraditional students. We recognize that today's colleges consist of more and more students who see landing a good job as a watermark in their lives.

Table 1. America's Top Stressful Occupations

OCCUPATIONS	STRESS INDICATORS
1. Firefighter	Stress Rank (200), Stress Score (111), Hours per day (11)
2. Corporate Executive	Stress Rank (199), Stress Score (109), Hours per day (11)
3. Taxi Drive	Stress Rank (198), Stress Score (100), Hours per day (9.5)
4. Surgeon	Stress Rank (197), Stress Score (99), Hours per day (11)
5. Police Officer	Stress Rank (196), Stress Score (94), Hours per day (9.5)
6. Commercial Pilot	Stress Rank (195), Stress Score (85), Hours per day (9)
7. Highway Patrol Officer	Stress Rank (194), Stress Score (81), Hours per day (9.5)
8. Public Relations Officer	Stress Rank (193), Stress Score (79), Hours per day (9)
9. Advertising Executive	Stress Rank (192), Stress Score (75), Hours per day (9.5)
10. Real Estate Agent	Stress Rank (191), Stress Score (73), Hours per day (9.5)

Source: CareerCast.com

The implication of this situation is troubling for a predominate number of college graduates. The rise of temporary employment may not be enough for many high achievers.[7] In fact, some students

---

7 *"More temp workers are becoming permanent," by Paul Davidson*

are already losing hope in getting a good job. The book is especially designed for frustrated parents, anxious students, bewildered professors and educators, and those who deeply care for college graduates. We offer sound, proven, and practical strategies to help increase the chances of being considered for job openings. Many of these principles are life experiences and lessons that usually develop into a natural approach and lifestyle, to be used throughout one's career. Therefore, being successful depends on understanding your own strength and weaknesses, recognizing the economic climate, and then developing and implementing an attractive and operative strategy that best suits you. Regardless of your age, experience, or job market, you *can* be successful.

"If your actions inspire others to dream more, learn more, do more and become more, you are a leader."

JOHN QUINCY ADAMS

1

Market Trends for the 21st Century

A Landscape of Doom

For many people, the bad economic picture will not change soon enough. According to a USA Today/Gallup Poll, almost three-fourths of those surveyed don't like what's going on in the country.[8] David Walker, the former Chief of the Government Accountable Office, predicts a poorer America if the economy doesn't change: "We've kicked the can down the road as far as we can. We are at the abyss."[9] Economic turbulence has overtaken our dreams of the American Dream. Economic turbulence relates to the chaos that now plaques our financial institutions, wreaking havoc on our normalcy. With a weak job growth, many U.S. jobs will continue to be outsourced globally or automated through technology. In fact, the government estimates that an additional 1.2 million manufacturing jobs will disappear by 2018.[10] In this economic downturn, many people are just happy to have *a* job.

Yet, the hectic work environment creates severe consequences to today's workers as well. According to the Conference Board research group, only 45% of Americans are satisfied with their work.[11] This situation fosters an environment of emotionally drained folks. According to a CareerBuilder.com survey, one-half of workers reported that they feel a great deal of stress on the job.[12] Ultimately, this hectic environment is destroying family life. Forty-four percent of working moms admitted being preoccupied with work while at home; thirty-six percent of working dads reported they bring work home at least once a week. It is evident that too many people remain in jobs they hate because of the financial gain. Unfortunately, some people even believe that chasing these financial goals will produce happiness.

8   "In America' next decade, change and challenges," by Rick Hampson
9   "In America' next decade, change and challenges," by Rick Hampson
10 "In America' next decade, change and challenges," by Rick Hampson
11 "U.S. job satisfaction at lowest levels in two decades," by The Conference Board
12 "CareerBuilder survey finds growing worker disenchantment, long hours and stress" by Careerbuilder.com

Workers now feel trapped by the current economy. In this scenario, an individual is so desperate to find "any" job that once they're on board, they pray that the organization will help them with their career advancement if they work hard. However, many bosses either undervalue or underdevelop their employees. These same managers may be great at completing work tasks but neglect mentoring and/or equipping their workforce to be as successful. This speaks to issues of working in a "dead-end" job.[13]

Following emerging trends may assist individuals in grasping what's happening and understanding how to better prepare for their future pursuits (see Table 2). One of the critical factors in the job market is globalization as well as the demographic changes. Dr. James H. Johnson, Jr. of the University of North Carolina predicts significant changes in America: "Within the next five years, we are going to see this huge wave of retirements. Behind the Baby Boom, Americans stopped having children in sufficient numbers to replace ourselves… The only way to meet our labor needs in the future will be through some combination of new immigrants and global recruitment." Driving market forces such as globalization are key factors in understanding the economic challenges faced by the nation. Yet, understanding what is happening across the world can provide more opportunities for landing the 'right' job.

---

13 *"How to overcome burnout from a dead end job," by Daryl D. Green*

Table 2. Global Trend Watch List

- **Globalization** – The global financial crisis has reinforced the interconnectedness of the world's economies. One nation's economic troubles can easily impact another country across the globe. For example, global outsourcing affects every nation. According to the Forrester Research, approximately 3.3 million U.S. jobs and $136 billion in wages could be moved overseas to countries like India or China by 2015.

- **The Age of the Part-time Worker** – Charles Handy, author of the *Age of Paradox*, predicts that we are witnessing the end of the full-time employee. Workers will become independent contractors. In December of 2008, part-time workers for economic reasons rose to over 8 million according to the US Bureau of Labor and Statistics (BLS).

- **Multicultural Workforce** - According to the BLS, minorities and immigrants will constitute a larger share of the population while White, non-Hispanic persons will decrease in the labor force, falling from 69% percent in 2006 to 64.6 % in 2016. Additionally, the number of women in the workforce will grow at a slightly faster rate than men.

- **Quest for Global Talent** - With globalization, there has been a search for talent everywhere. In this scenario, many countries will actively recruit talent from across the globe. Thus, removing the continental borders of countries trying to protect homegrown talent.

- **Technological Advances** – Technology will continue to influence social networks and relationships. For example, mobile technologies such as cell phones and PDFs have changed how most Americans communicate with each other.

- **Social Networking** – According to comScore Report, in June 2008, social networking total audience grew 64 million (12%) which was over twice as fast as the total Internet audience. Facebook.com is the largest social network in the world at 132 million.

- **Lifetime Learning** – Lifetime learning is a reality for future opportunities and career advancement. For the past several years, online enrollment have been growing substantially faster than traditional educational enrollment. According to estimates, over 3.9 million students took at least one online course in the fall 2007 term. Online learning is flexible, self-paced, and readily accessible to students.

A Brighter Day for Employment

Looking toward the future, many students should focus on brighter days ahead for near-term employment. In fact, the current indicators are showing the economy may be turning around. According to the US Labor Department predictions for 2008 through 2018, the economy is estimated to generate over 15 million jobs (with a total employment of 152 million in 2018).[14] Although the manufacturing and construction industries will continue to take a beating, there are promising industries such as consulting, computer systems design, and employment services. Combined these fields are projected to produce over 2 million jobs by 2018.[15] Yet, there are other good industries which include science and technology; healthcare; business and finance; education and civics; arts and science.[16]

Yet, this transition to a better economy is not without problems. There will be pressures to continue to flatten organizations with outsourcing and automation. These corporate initiatives may be linked to the shrinking of middle class families. An economist from MIT commented in an article, "I think we'll see continued growth of very high- and relatively low-skilled jobs at the expense of the middle."[17] He argues this will challenge future organizations to stabilize their workforce. Yet, prepared individuals understand these obstacles and accept them with a genuine optimism, knowing that brighter days are ahead.

---

14 *"A job seeker's glimpse into the crystal ball," by Liz Wolgemuth*
15 *"A job seeker's glimpse into the crystal ball," by Liz Wolgemuth*
16 *"America's best careers," by Liz Wolgemuth*
17 *"A job seeker's glimpse into the crystal ball," by Liz Wolgemuth*

"And first and foremost, your education can fortify you against the uncertainties of a 21st century economy."

PRESIDENT BARACK OBAMA

· · · · · · · · · · · · · · · ·

**HAMPTON UNIVERSITY
COMMENCEMENT 2010**

2

A Vocation in Life

Unfortunately, there are millions of employees who have jobs that do not energize them. If a person feels under-utilize in his or her organization, it is difficult to be passionate about it. Based on several consultations by Dr. Green, several interviewees indicated that "It is difficult to make it to the next day in this situation." It's apparent that on a routine basis, many employees force themselves to work without a clear purpose. Many people are succeeding in the corporate environment while failing miserably at their personal relationships. It is the sentiment of many workers that they are 'underutilized' and 'wasted' in their organizations. Consequently, they are never able to showcase their natural abilities and skills. They are caught in a corporate prison where there is no escape. These workers exist in hopelessness and are on a fast track toward being burnt out. This reality has not gone unnoticed and is a far cry from what the passionate career minded individual's experience should be.

Numerous people work to maintain their daily bread without ever doing what they love. Marci Alboher, author of *One Person, Multiple Careers*, examines this reality: "Sometimes taking yourself off the fast track in your primary career opens the door to building a second one…you might avoid the burnout and narrowness of the focus that often plaque the highest achievers in a given field."[18] Sadly, many managers are unable to inspire today's workforce toward greater performance. Management guru Peter Drucker argued for several decades that managers must understand their employees as well as their customers.[19] Few executives listened. Drucker concluded, "Business tends to drift from leadership to mediocrity. And the mediocre is three-quarters down the road to being marginal." Yet, emerging leaders need to know how to rekindle such emotions in the workplace. The point here is that one's passion or calling can transform an individual's work life which will subsequently improve a business' organizational performance.

Becoming more productive in life is a function of working in a

---

18 *One Person, Multiple Careers by Marci Alboher*
19 *The Essential Drucker by Peter Drucker*

career that is aligned with one's abilities. Unfortunately, many organizations fail to understand this simple principle. As a consequence, their employees are in jobs that do not fit their abilities. Yes, the organization may know the individual's education and career experience; however, managers are unable to understand the worker's ability without properly evaluating the worker's performance and receiving input from that worker. There is a distinct difference between an occupation and a vocation. An occupation relates to the principal activity in an individual's life that earns money for living.

Some people, due to their own financial situation, are forced to work in jobs they hate. Others must occupy jobs where they are overqualified; this speaks to the issue of underemployment in our nation. Yet, many folks are 'slaves' to their jobs simply because of the income they provide. This situation can lead to stress, depression, and unhappiness. In fact, some people take desperate measures. According to one study, more than 30,000 Americans take their lives annually.[20] This works out to more than three suicides for every two murders, nationally. A vocation is considered a worker's natural alignment with one's ability. Vocation relates to a career which a person is particularly suited or qualified to perform. Some individuals credit this special alignment to a divine providence. In the medieval Christian period, it was believed that God called certain people and their work was a 'calling.' This calling was usually reserved for the clergy and priest. In the secular sense, individuals who can fully use all of their talents in a way that liberates them can make great contributions to society. In fact, these individuals can create jobs that previously did not exist (see Figure 1).[21] However, it does invoke a different mental journey. Marsha Sinetar, author of *Do What You Love, The Money Will Follow*, argues that individuals rarely take the time for introspection: "Most of us think about our jobs or our careers as a means to fulfill responsibilities to families and creditors, to gain more material comforts, and to

---

20 *"Suicide prevention campaign is unveiled," by The New York Times*
21 *"10 careers that didn't exist 10 years ago" by Rachel Zupek*

achieve status and recognition. But we pay a high price for this kind of thinking."[22] This mental awakening is happening across the nation. Thus, some people are able to tap into their own 'calling.' Therefore, it is important that individuals take the time to learn what they enjoy and what they are good at. This reality will lead them to their special vocation. In fact, one has a calling when he or she realizes what can be done with his or her God-given abilities. Once this career revelation is realized, typically an individual can mentally take the journey toward greater happiness and job performance.

22 *Do What You Love, The Money Will Follow by Marsha Sinetar*

Figure 1. Emerging Careers of the Future

JOBS
1. **Blogger** – provides information to online audiences in a conversational style, showcasing his or her expertise.
2. **Content or Community Manager** – can manage a website or serve as a liaison between company and the public.
3. **Green Funeral Director** – meets the funeral service needs of their clients in an environmentally conscious way.
4. **Interior Redesigner** – remodels homes using materials already available to their customers.
5. **Patient Advocate** – works in the best interest of the patient in securing the customer's medical needs.
6. **Senior Move Management** – assists seniors and their families in transitioning to the next stages of their living.
7. **Social Media Strategist** – uses social media tools to better position his or her clients.
8. **User Experience Analyst** – explores effective ways to make websites or other online experiences better.
9. **Video Journalist** – adapts to reporting and using video to convey the latest news.
10. **Virtual Business Service Provider** – seeks to provide businesses services that are needed to operate an online operation.

Source: "10 careers that didn't exist 10 years ago" by Rachel Zupek

As societal norms lead people to acquire more things in order to secure happiness, individuals can become very unhappy with life in general. It is important that individuals take a personal assessment of their own career objectives in conjunction with their own calling. High performance organizations incorporate this factor of human capital variable in their corporate strategies. Therefore, organizations that understand how to tap into an employee's calling will have a competitive advantage because they will maximize the talents of their workforce. Strategically, there will be a global war for top worker talent. Businesses that understand this fact will continue to have sustainable growth. Those that miss it will be at a clear competitive disadvantage. Consider companies like Google, Southwest Airlines, and the like. These are companies with high performing talent that affects their bottom-line.

"A man always has two reasons for the things he does
—a good one and the real one."

JP MORGAN

3

Corporate Expectations for Workers

Many employers have critical expectations for future workers that are not being fulfilled. Sadly, most employees cannot understand it since they have suffered severely. Job satisfaction for today's employees continues to tank.[23] Therefore, some students are graduating from universities but are unable to compete for jobs due to the lack of their understanding of organizations' expectations. In fact, many adults are learning the hard way that a bachelor's or a master's degree doesn't guarantee them a good job.[24] In fact, employers are expecting a lot out of today's workforce. According to a recent IBM's survey of 1,500 chief executives, employers are shifting their views of what corporate values are important. [25]

In fact, CEOs in the survey ranked creativity as the most important leadership competency over operational effectiveness, influence, and dedication. Even under distress, businesses understand they must do something different to survive. Therefore, organizations want self-starters who are internally driven and add value to the company instead of just being "dead weight." Some of the other attributes include critical thinking, flexible, creative, good communication, and adaptable to changing circumstances. Columnist Rick Newman argues, "The real payoff goes to people with an ever expanding set of skills who work in growing and complex fields. The highest earners are well educated, but they also have strong 'tacit' and cognitive' skills that are difficult to teach in the classroom: informed intuition, judgment under pressure, the ability to solve problems that don't have obvious solution."[26] Unfortunately, most people are not prepared for the future economy. According to a McKinsey survey, 71% of Americans work in jobs (blue and white collar) where there is a low demand from employers or an oversupply of labor.[27] Therefore, the increased income will go to individuals who are engaged in growing industries that require specialized skill sets.

---

23 *"CareerBuilder survey finds growing worker disenchantment, long hours and stress," by CareerBuilder*
24 *"Surviving the American makeover," by Rick Newman*
25 *"What chief executives really wanty" by Frank Kern*
26 *"Surviving the American makeover," by Rick Newman*
27 *"Surviving the American makeover," by Rick Newman*

Some universities understand that their programs must better prepare their students for the corporate world if they want them to be competitive. The economic picture has caused many organizations to reduce their presences in universities across the nation. To a shrewd executive, it probably doesn't make sense to hire young graduates when the economic picture for the company may be uncertain. Only 2 industry sectors expect to add more jobs, in education, health, and government in the near term. However, some companies feel their support to academic institutions make business sense since it demonstrates the organizations' social responsibility to their communities. Furthermore, some universities have been too busy attempting to shore up their economic woes to pay attention to other organizations. Yet, there are some bright signs.

Winston-Salem State University (WSSU), one of the 16 constituents of the University of North Carolina, continues to make a high commitment to furthering alliances with the public and private institutions. The university is an active member of the National Urban League's Black Executive Exchange Program (BEEP). BEEP has a historical record of over 40 years working in partnership with corporations, government agencies, non-profits, and other institutions where black executives serve as "Visiting Professors" at primarily black colleges. The program provides students with an opportunity to ask questions and gain insight into how to compete in corporate America.

Corporate professions are a part of WSSU's strategy to make their students competitive. In March of 2010, WSSU hosted a variety of organizations to connect with their students; the organizations included UPS, Central Intelligence Agency, Department of Energy, and Oak Ridge National Laboratory. LaMonica Singleton, WSSU Director of Career Services, understands the importance of students making a connection with corporate America: "Students can relate to individuals who have been where they are. Students can listen and relate to the professionals." She further notes that students see positive role models and can see themselves personally in a different setting." Kevin Bryant, a WSSU junior from Goldsboro, North Carolina, sees the value in having professions coming to campus: "I think it's important for students to broaden their horizons. Having this exposure is important." Bryant further adds that these professionals gave him a dose of reality regarding how the corporate world operates.

Unfortunately, the current economic turbulence makes it difficult for college students to be optimistic. However, having a good plan can increase the odds for most students in landing a good job. Therefore, understanding what future employers expect and networking with corporate professionals are critical factors in navigating the current economic turbulence.

"Having a purpose to your life: Purpose does not mean having a job."
DR. MAYA ANGELOU

• • • • • • • • • • • • • • •

4

Job Strategies for the Future

Even in economic turbulence, opportunities will present themselves. Therefore, individuals must be flexible in using the right job strategies. Opportunities will present themselves in some form in the future. With globalization, there has been a search for talent everywhere. Authors Christiane Kupysch and Pang Eng Fong explain that many countries have begun to actively recruit foreign talent or encourage their own citizens to return to their respective countries to help them compete.[28] Therefore, college students need to be proactive about landing a job. Students should consider their personal brand. They need to act and behave in ways that demonstrate good character to their potential employer. Derrick Craver, Vice President - South Zone Strategic Accounts for UPS, argues that students need to take advantage of opportunities in brand building: "How to carry yourself in a day-to-day situation is important." He notes work ethic as an example. "It starts by coming to work on time." Everything you do will be a reflection of your brand. Therefore, planning becomes a part of the secret in today's employment. Unfortunately, many students do not realize that having a job strategy is critical (Figure 2).

---

28 *"Competing for Global Talent", by Christiane Kupysch and Pang Eng Fong*

Figure 2. Critical Job Strategies for the Future

- **Branding.** Define, promote, and protect your image online and off-line. Never dress inappropriately in a business setting or showcase a less flattering image on social networks like MySpace, for future employers to view.

- **Communications.** Become an effective communicator (oral and written).

- **Critical Thinking.** Take courses that require you to think critically and logically about problems. Today's employers are looking for innovators and creators, not just employees.

- **Current & well-versed.** Stay abreast of current news and issues nationally and globally while reading appropriate industry publications.

- **Flexibility.** Be mobile and adaptable to moving away from your comfort zone and into other areas of the world to gain experience.

- **Global Citizen.** Globalization represents the future. Study abroad and develop another language to be competitive internationally as well as locally.

- **Job Homework.** Study potential employers and their problems before an interview.

- **Leadership.** Get involved in organizations on campus and in your community where you can showcase your leadership. By serving others, you are building character for your next career.

- **Love & Passion.** Pursue a career that you love and you will never work another day in your life because your work will speak to who you are as an individual and not just a job.

- **Networking.** Begin to build a professional network by talking to individuals within your industry. Find a mentor or advisor who is willing to assist you in developing your career strategy.

- **Opportunity.** Be aware of opportunities and be prepared to act quickly on them.

- **Seasoned Worker.** Seek to obtain work experience through co-ops and internships to build corporate experience. If a job is not available, volunteer to help an organization and grow your expertise.

- **Uniqueness.** Develop a unique skill or talent that is very valuable in your discipline.

However, one of the most important points to learn is that the job search is a process. This process takes a lot of time and effort, and its success culminates with the job offer. Traditionally, this process consists of the three major steps: data and information gathering, preparation, and relationships. No one is a master at all three, but if you can perform well in two of three areas, you can greatly increase your chance for success. We'll address these topics in a rapid fire session. Additionally, a more detailed list of job strategies can be found in Appendix C.

Information Gain or Drain?

Often in work environments, people are heard saying, "Information is power." We all said, "Just think if I knew more, or knew then what I know now, I would have made better decisions." This is true in work and in life. Fortunately for you, you know more about *you* than any one on the planet, and that makes *you* an expert. This is what a recruiter or potential employee wants to know. It's your job to put *yourself* on display. It's not just about your skills and education. It is also how well you will fit into an organization and be a benefit to the team. To learn more about yourself there are useful tools available to help you take a personal inventory – a personal self – assessment, or even a peer review. These will aid you in finding your passion, strengths, weaknesses, likes and dislikes. It's important to understanding your personality traits and how you would perform in stressful situations, or working with people, etc. These are things employees are looking to learn about *you*, and these are things you should share in an interview.

The Time is Coming!

Hopefully, while in college, you've been honing your skills and mastering your craft. Certainly, that's what we do in college! We should further prepare for life after college by investing time (and possibly a little money) in our professional image. Your image comes in the form of a cover letter, resume, honing your communication skills, and your attire. There was a student who was able to conduct a "90 second interview" with a recruiter, between scheduled back-to-back interviews. All of which occurred before the next interviewee walked in to be greeted, simply because of a professionally formatted resume. Now that's selling yourself – even when you're left off the interview list. Don't overlook any of these crucial steps, they could make all the difference between you and the next interviewee! If you're concerned about your resume, there are things you can do about it.

To avoid employment gaps consider activities that you continued to participate in during that gap in time, and add them to your resume. If you are currently in a gap, fill it with something meaningful. Here's an idea – start a blog or a newsletter, or submit articles in your field. Some people call it research! Now, by doing so, it will keep you occupied and sane, all at the same time while you're looking to land a job. While in college, you may have participated in an internship program or work program through your school to gain some experience in your field. If not, all is not lost. You can create your own experience through volunteer work, or hiring yourself as an entrepreneur starting out with small projects in your field. Remember – you have a degree now!

Go Fetch!

One of the most popular radio talk show personalities in America is Dave Ramsey, host of *The Dave Ramsey Show*. One of his favorite lines to callers goes something like, "Now it's time to leave the cave, kill something and drag it home …" That's the attitude needed to be successful.[29] Although you've collected job opening information from newspapers, magazines, and the web, there are other sources to consider. As an alum, you can revisit your school's career placement center. See who was on campus recently, recruiters, sponsors for campus programs and activities, and others who are familiar with your school and its students. They may have newer openings that just became available since graduating, who knows? The whole point is you have to be dogmatic in hunting down your first prey when you're outside your cave! Be dogmatic!

Work the Net

Networking – this is where the real opportunities are found. A layman's definition of networking is gaining access to those who know where the jobs are, and can talk with someone about it. If you think about it, of everyone who's *ever* gotten a job, you'll notice that there was always one thing they all had in common - someone gave them a shot! Oh, sure that person had skills and experience, but that's only part of it. Skills and experience can come a-dime-a-dozen, particularly in some markets. Yet, they were all given a shot. Your job is to get them to give you a shot. Maybe they knew a mutual friend, or someone wanting to help someone down on their luck, or someone met someone just the other day…, and they GAVE them A SHOT. Bill Washington, Vice President, Strategic Account Sales for UPS, explains the importance of good networks: "Align yourself with your network and set goals." That's a big part of networking – making a connection! Building relationships will get you a job that's not advertised, that only one or two people in the whole company know

---

29 *Financial Peace by Dave Ramsey*

anything about. There are associations, civil community events, and local clubs, where sometimes job opportunities are discussed and discovered. Unfortunately, if they don't know you, or your interests, or skills, or hobbies, then there's no connection, no opportunity.

Today's college students cannot afford to use traditional strategies in hopes of landing a good job. Economic troubles in our nation and abroad continue to create an unstable and unpredictable job market. Parents across this country tell their children "get a good education and you will get a good job." However, in this economic rollercoaster, this is not always true. US manufacturing jobs continue to evaporate as global outsourcing becomes the norm for businesses that seek to increase their profits. Under more economic pressures than ever, individuals need to refocus their strategies as they witness the last era of uncertainty.[30] In Appendix C, there is an extensive list of job strategies.

A Word of Caution

Be very mindful not to set too lofty goals when attempting to get your foot in the door, yet see it as an opportunity! Organizations are looking for employees who are great communicators who can convey critical messages to different audiences and still be effective. That's what we're after here, an opportunity. Have some flexibility throughout this process. For example, students should consider internships. David Milan, Emergency Management Group Leader at Oak Ridge National Laboratory has been involved in recruiting new hires, visiting colleges and universities, and mentoring students for over 10 years. At 57 years old, Milan has a wealth of experience to offer. He encourages "internships; a good resume; networking; don't limit the employment search to one specific business sector."

Consider large corporations or even small mom and pop organizations, either part-time or contract work. Opportunities can be found everywhere. Derrick Craver, Vice President - South Zone Strategic

30 *Breaking Organizational Ties by Daryl D. Green*

Accounts for UPS, explains, "An education is the foundation [for opportunities]." Bill Washington, Vice President, Strategic Account Sales for UPS, argues that having a plan is critical for taking advantage of opportunities: "In any area of life, it's important to have a roadmap." He encourages developing a 1 to 3 year plan to reach goals. Some have been employed as walk-ins or by going overseas – you only live once! Craver shares how flexibility can assist an individual's career. Loaded with a college degree, Derrick spent his early years at UPS loading trucks and driving them. This reality meant doing things he did not want to do and was overqualified to perform. Yet, it paid off. Derrick notes, "I came a long way. I was never afraid of hard work." In the end, with persistence, you will get to where you want to go, with time and patience, and of course with more opportunities.

"It is not how long you live that counts but what you do in your life that is important. You've got to learn how to deal with the storms of life."
REV. RICHARD BROWN, JR.

5

Conclusion

"So education is what has always allowed us to meet the challenges of a changing world…You're entering a job market, in an era of heightened international competition, with an economy that's still rebounding from the worst crisis since the Great Depression," echoed President Barak Obama to a group of hopeful graduates at Hampton University in Virginia.[31] It will be a feat with much difficulty. During these times of rapid change and financial turmoil, college students are looking for any angle to assist them in getting the right job. In the near-term, economic turbulence will be a critical factor for most institutions. Given this reality, some individuals looking at future market trends may become fearful.[32] In fact, others may even feel pessimistic about near-term career opportunities. Yet, hope is not lost if people are prepared for the future. However, it may take operating outside of your comfort zone including extending your network beyond your current friendship circles.[33]

Here's what it takes …
You must, first and foremost, know what your career interests are *and* why! Think of it this way, most recruiters or employers will not only ask, but the good ones, the ones you really want to work for will really want to know why. They want to hear a story, a really good story about your passion. Much has already been written about how successful and happy people are when they pursue their passions. Employers and researchers know this, and look to hire as many passionate employees as they possibly can. Passionate employees are more than productive employees. They live it! They eat it up! Remember when you were starting out as a new college student? Your major field of study was an attraction for you (when you finally decided on a major!). You were relieved, yet regardless of the extra work outside of our interest, it sometimes requires, the attraction still remained. It should be the same now – when it's time to pursue that career. Guess what? There really is no difference between you or your employer. Put yourself in their shoes. If you owned the

---

31 "Obama to Hampton University graduates: 'be role models for your brothers and sisters'" by Samieh Shalash
32 Anatomy of a Trend by Henrik Vejlgaard
33 "Job Search Strategies in Tough Economic Times," by Arizona State University

company, would you be passionate about the products or services you offer? Why – because they are a representation of you, as well as the success of the organization. You would do all you possibly could to be successful. It all comes from the passion on the inside. So here's the big clue: Know your passion! Did you know the word passion is a derivative of the word interest? Interest speaks to who you are. It's not what you studied! Shift your focus from your degree to your passion, definitely not vice versa.

Secondly, do your due diligence. Take the necessary time, maybe at your leisure, to stay abreast of the new developments, trends, and challenges in your career field. Study all the ins and outs surrounding the career path you are about to pursue. So many times students neglect the value of this minor detail. If it's a passion, this should come with ease. With heavy course loads and demanding instructors, creating time for this can be difficult, but when you make it a lifestyle, play in it! The goal is to plan today as if you're interviewing tomorrow! Think of the Warner Brothers cartoon of the Coyote and the Roadrunner. If you ask Mr. Wile E. Coyote why does he "give chase" to the roadrunner, he'll tell you, "Why of course, this is what I (love to) do!" But, if you follow him back to the cave; you'll see it's also what he's been planning to do, too. This point is to plan, plan, and plan.

Lastly, make the best out of every opportunity. How can you do this when all you have to show on your resume is delivering pizzas while in college!? Here's one example of how to make the best of your life's experiences: Say Joe College Student is delivering pizzas and studying finance over at the Local State University, yet his dream is to become a Wall Street whiz after graduating from college. He makes the best of it through his resume! Not only did this experience put a little bit of money in his pocket while in school, more importantly it helped to build a case for him toward his career. How would you make the case? Check it out: Obviously, the company found him to be trustworthy, competent, and punctual, or else he wouldn't have kept the job for very long. From a financial standpoint,

Joe is managing and handling cash receipts. His sleepy roommate may laugh at Joe's convenient part-time pizza job, but when these two finance majors graduate, who would you hire? Can you say the same about yourself in an interview? Are you 'trustworthy, competent, and punctual?' This is what most bosses want to hear. In this example, pizza is the difference, and Joe can unashamedly prove it! And, that's not mentioning the added fact thatJoe signs a personal financial statement and time sheet at the end of each shift. Who would you hire? Many would choose Pizza Joe every time – and so would you!

A pizza delivery job and a career in finance, on the surface it doesn't connect, unless you connect them. Although this example may be a stretch, the point is Joe made the best of it. Whether it was his past or current work experience, skills, and abilities, any of these can be used as a stepping stone, supporting you in your pursuits. So, what have you done in the past, or are doing today that will prepare you for the job of your dreams? There is always an option or an alternative to every situation, if it's not a job, how about previous volunteer work, or civil roles and responsibilities? Any of these things can be a benefit to you in an interview and is a part of your story.

Unfortunately, few colleges can keep us abreast of the many changes taking place in the job search market. Typically, every year since the first Gulf War under President Clinton, the job search for new graduates has been difficult (although there were a few good years during the dot com craze). Therefore, it is important to get advice from individuals who are currently in the hiring market, helping college students and seasoned employees find gainful employment. In fact, few books focus on the needs of today's college graduate. This book provides students a systematic approach to dealing with this uncertainty. Landing a 'good' job requires special character, persistence, commitment, passion, and vision to become successful. By taking control of your career strategy, college students can make a positive step in navigating these difficult economic times and landing their future jobs. Start today and achieve your desired outcome!

The ultimate measure of a man is not where he stands in moments of comfort and convenience, but where he stands at times of challenge and controversy.

- MARTIN LUTHER KING, JR.,

CIVIL RIGHTS LEADER

Chapter Notes

Introduction

Bureau of Labor Statistics website: http://www.bls.gov/news.
release/empsit.nr0.htm.

Choy, Susan. "Findings from the condition of education 2002:
Nontraditional Undergraduates." National Center for Education
Statistics. (2002). http://nces.ed.gov/pubs2002/2002012.pdf
(accessed 8 May 2010).

CNBC.com. "America's most stressful jobs in 2010." (23 April 2010).
http://finance.yahoo.com/career-work/article/109379/americas-
most-stressful-jobs-2010?mod=career-worklife_balance (accessed
27 April 2010).

Davidson, Paul. "More temp workers are becoming permanent."
USA Today, (2010). http://www.usatoday.com/money/economy/
employment/2010-03-08-tempjobs08_ST_N.htm (accessed 26
April 2010).

Green, Daryl. "How to overcome burnout from a dead end
job." *Associatedcontent.com*. (18 August 2008). http://www.
associatedcontent.com/article/962950/how_to_overcome_
burnout_from_a_dead.html?cat=31 (accessed 3 October 2009).

U.S. Department of Education. "Federal student aid." National
Center for Education Statistics. (2002). http://studentaid.ed.gov/
PORTALSWebApp/students/english/aboutus.jsp (accessed 8 May
2010).

Wolgemuth, Liz. (March 2010). "A job seeker's glimpse into the
crystal ball." *U.S. News & World Report*.

Wolgemuth, Liz. (May 2010). "America's best careers." *U.S. News &
World Report*.

CHAPTER 1

Green, Daryl. "How to overcome burnout from a dead end job." *Associatedcontent.com*. (18 August 2008). http://www. associatedcontent.com/article/962950/how_to_overcome_ burnout_from_a_dead.html?cat=31 (accessed 3 October 2009).

Hampson, Rick. "In America's next decade, change and challenges." *USA Today*, (2010). http://www.usatoday.com/news/nation/2010-01-04-2020-the-next-decade_N.htm (accessed 26 April 2010).

CHAPTER 2

Alboher, Marci. *One Person, Multiple Careers*. New York, NY: Warner Books, 2007.

CNBC.com. "America's most stressful jobs in 2010." (23 April 2010). http://finance.yahoo.com/career-work/article/109379/americas-most-stressful-jobs-2010?mod=career-worklife_balance (accessed 27 April 2010).

Drucker, Peter. *The Essential Drucker: The Best of Sixty Years of Peter Drucker's Essential Writings on Management*. New York, NY: HarperCollins Publishers, Inc, 2001.

Sinetar, Marsha. *Do What You Love, the Money Will Follow: Discovering Your Right Livelihood*, New York: Dell, 1989.

The New York Times. "Suicide prevention campaign is unveiled." (3 May 2001). http://www.nytimes.com/2001/05/03/us/suicide-prevention-campaign-is-unveiled.html (accessed 28 April 2010).

Zupek, Rachel. "10 careers that didn't exist 10 years ago." *CareerBuilder.com*, (2010). http://msn.careerbuilder.com/Article/ MSN-2126-Job-Info-and-Trends-10-Careers-That-Didnt-Exist-10-

Years-Ago/?ArticleID=2126&cbRecursionCnt=1&cbsid=cdde9be
563d446bfaa44d15513b20ce1-325494581-wg-6 (accessed 26 April
2010).

CHAPTER 3

Careerbuilder.com. "CareerBuilder survey finds growing worker
disenchantment, long hours and stress." http://www.careerbuilder.
com/share/aboutus/pressreleasesdetail.aspx?id=pr018&sd=8%2f
30%2f2001&ed=12%2f31%2f2001&cbRecursionCnt=1&cbsid=6
893903c966c47b093776033d7eca2d5-328021154-RR-4 (24 May
2010).

Kern, Frank. (19 May 2010). "What chief executives really
want." *Yahoo! Finance.* http://finance.yahoo.com/career-work/
article/109596/what-chief-executives-really-want?mod=career-
leadership (24 May 2010).

Newman, Rick. (March 2010). "Surviving the American makeover,
U.S. News & World Report.

The Conference Board. "U.S. job satisfaction at lowest levels in two
decades." Press Release (5 January 2010). http://www.conference-
board.org/utilities/pressdetail.cfm?press_id=3820 (24 May 2010).

CHAPTER 4

Green, Daryl. *Breaking Organizational Ties.* United States of
America: CreateSpace Publisher, 2010.

Kuptsch, Christiane & Eng Fong Pang. *Competing for Global Talent.*
Geneva: International Labour Office and Wee Kim Wee Centre,
2006.

Ramsey, Dave. *Financial Peace.* Nashville, TN: Lampo Press, 1995.

Conclusion

Arizona State University. "Job search strategies in tough economic times." (2010). http://students.asu.edu/career/strategies_article (accessed 27 April 2010).

Shalash, Samieh. "Obama to Hampton University graduates: 'be role models for your brothers and sisters.'" (10 May 2010). http://articles.dailypress.com/2010-05-10/news/dp-local_hu-obama-speech_0510may10_1_role-models-graduates-barack-obama (accessed 10 May 2010).

Vejlgaard, Henrik. *Anatomy of a Trend*. New York: McGraw-Hill, 2008.

WTKR. "Transcript of President Barack Obama's commencement address to Hampton University." (10 May 2010). http://www.wtkr.com/news/wtkr-obama-hampton-address-transcript,0,7478536.story?page=1 (accessed 10 May 2010).

About the Author

Dr. Daryl D. Green is a modern day strategist and a nationally recognized lecturer. Dr. Green loves developing intellectual properties to assist individuals with making better decisions. He is an adjunct professor at Lincoln Memorial University. He has also been a faculty member at Knoxville College. He has over 20 years of assisting organizations and individuals with making good decisions.

Currently, Dr. Green is the author of several books and writes a syndicated online column on contemporary issues where over 3,000 online publishers/content providers around the globe have used his articles. His *FamilyVision* column syndicated through the Newspaper Publishers Association reached over 200 newspapers and more than 15 million readers across the country. Additionally, Dr. Green has been noted and quoted by *USA Today, Ebony Magazine,* and the *Associated Press.* He has also been a freelance writer and guest columnist for various publications, including *Knoxville News Sentinel, Knoxville Enlightener, Discovery Magazine,* and the *IEEE Technology and Society Magazine.* He has also been a special assignment reporter for the *BIG Bulletin/ Reporter.*

His professional experience includes management, engineering, research and development, marketing, and personal coaching. He received a B.S. in mechanical engineering and an MA in Organizational Management. Dr. Green received a doctoral degree in strategic leadership from Regent University. He is a past talk show host, a nationally recognized lecturer, nationally syndicated columnist, and personal advisor. Before his 30th birthday, he had already managed over 400 projects, estimated at $100 million dollars. These experiences place him in a unique position for understanding emerging trends. If you would like him to speak to your organization or would like more information about his company services, please contact:

PMLA
P.O. Box 32733
Knoxville, TN 37930-2733
Phone: (865) 602-7858
Email: advice@darylgreen.org
Home page: www.darylgreen.org

William Bailey has earned a master's degree in business administration from Liberty University, and a civil engineering degree from North Carolina A&T State University. His expertise is in the areas of project management, contract administration, and cost and risk avoidance. Having developed strategic acquisition plans for major systems for government contracting activities for the US Department of Energy for over ten years, William understands the nature of complex problems. Previously, he was employed with other government agencies including: the Maryland State Highway Administration and the North Carolina Department of Transportation. He has credentialed as a Project Management Professional, from the Project Management Institute, and as a Registered Environmental Manager with the National Registry of Environmental Managers. For several years, William has volunteered as a visiting professor and lecturer at local educational and church events in the Knoxville, Tennessee metropolitan area. Today, he serves as volunteer to youth ministries at Grace Baptist Church in the Karns area.

Readers' Suggestions & Input

Our company is constantly updating our products so that they are accurate and relevant. If you find missing information, want to to provide some suggestions, or need additional information, please write, fax, or email us at:

PMLA
P.O. Box 32733
Knoxville, TN 37930-2733
Fax: (865) 602-7858
Email: pmla@att.net

Other Books by Dr. Green

Dr. Green continues to research and produce information that seeks to better society. Below is a synopsis of some of his other products:

A Call to Destiny: How to Create Effective Ways to Assist Black Boys in America provides a practical assessment of what happens to young black boys in America. It seeks to provide ways for parents, educators, and supporters to assist these boys in their positive development. Without any intervention, young black boys, regardless of their social class, will not survive in the 21st century. In this book A Call to Destiny, you will (a) examine the severity of the problems facing young black boys, (b) learn new strategies to bring solutions to your child and the community at large, and (c) provide inspiration to continue the fight to save this generation of boys.
(**Paperback:** 50 pages, **ISBN-13:** 978-1442181021)

Awakening the Talents Within is a powerful, step by step approach that individuals can use to solve problems and contribute to their overall success. This book is a wake up call for the next generation of leaders. Green uses his charismatic style for today's hip hop culture, dealing with a wide range of issues from stopping procrastination to creating business ownership. The solutions contained in the book reflect over ten years of managing, consulting, and teaching in government, nonprofit, business, private and academic institutions.
(**Paperback:** 136 pages, **ISBN:** 978-0595146130, **Hardcover:** 140 pages, **ISBN:** 978-0595745722)

Book Publishing for Professionals provides the secrets of gaining this useful power. Packed with proven insights and advice, this book provides a simple, logical step for professionals. It includes effective writing tools, best publishing options, and marketing strategies to make your book successful in the marketplace. It is geared toward the writer who wants to write a non-fiction book (biography, cookbook, self-help, Christian book, textbook, etc.).
(**Paperback:** 68 pages, **ISBN:** 978-1449985561, Kindle: 68 ASIN: B0047T7DPA,**Hardcover:** 108 pages, **ISBN:** 978-0-557-98346-9, **DVD**: 26 minutes, **ASIN:** B001FB4Z3G, **CD**: 26 minutes, **ASIN:** B004CYFBBS)

Breaking Organizational Ties provides practical strategies for employees attempting to cope in jobs or environments which they hate. While most managers are only concerned with the bottom-line, they leave their employees vulnerable to the casualties of competitive markets. This book will enable readers to (a) learn how to survive and even enjoy your time at work even in a hostile environment, (b) gain greater confidence in your ability to grow while in a downsizing organization, and (c) discover the insight to go beyond your limitations by breaking the barriers of your self-doubt. (**Paperback:**124, **ISBN**: 978-1450511315, **Kindle:**124, **ASIN**: B003L77PBQ, **Hardcover:** 124 pages, ISBN: 978-0557388714)

More Than A Conqueror: Achieving Personal Fulfillment in Government Service is a message about how to take positive steps in achieving your goals while in government service. However, many individuals will be able to benefit from this book. In More than a Conqueror, you will (a) go beyond your self-imposed limitations by breaking the barrier of your self-doubt and (b) protect and cultivate your life in order to bring forth the best you can in your generation. (**Paperback**: 76 pages, **ISBN**: 978-0971400887)

My Cup Runneth Over: Setting Goals for Single Parents and Working Couples guides families in setting goals for themselves. Daryl and his wife have first-hand experience on this subject, both working full-time jobs, and raising three active children. This book uses a new management process called Meshing TM. The book is very different from most family books, focusing more on practical solutions. Daryl has used his experience as a manager from the government, nonprofit, and private business sectors to assist families in this country to do what we have done--take control of our family. Written in an informal, entertaining style, it provides information to families that give them HOPE. Creatively illustrated with graphics and charts, the book is also indexed for quick reference. It is essential reading for families in search of purpose.

Special Awards: January Book of the Month, The Larry Young Show 1998, Special Black History Award at Atkins Library, Featured on Heaven 600 (The Top Gospel Radio Station in the Country). (**Paperback:** 108 pages, **ISBN:** 978-1889745039, **Audiobook:** 978-1889745053, **Audio CD: ASIN:** B001VH787E)

Appendices

Job Strategy Resources – Appendix A

Top 2009 Employers for Entry Positions – Appendix B

50 Savvy Strategies for Gaining Employment – Appendix C

2010 Best Places to Live - Appendix D

Government Employment Abroad – Appendix E

Appendix A

JOB STRATEGY RESOURCES

Learn about information designed to assist college students with employment and career development. Contact the organizations for current information.

BOOKS/DOCUMENTS/WEBSITES

Career Resources

Can I Wear My Nose Ring to the Interview by Ellen Gordon Reeves

How'd You Score That Gig?: A Guide to the Coolest Jobs-and How to Get Them by Alexandra Levit

"How to Say It" by Rosalie Maggio

"Job Search Strategies of Recent Graduates" by Chris Bardwell

"Job Search Strategies in Tough Economic Times," by Arizona State University

Knock'em Dead 2010: The Ultimate Job Search Guide by Martin Yate

Knock'em Dead Cover Letters by Martin Yate

Knock'em Dead Resume by Martin Yate

The Complete Handbook of Modern Business Letters by Jack Griffin

The Don't Teach Corporate College by Alexandra Levit

What Color Is Your Parachute?2010: A Practical Manual for Job-Hunters and Career-Changers by Richard Nelson Bolles

Life Skills Resources

Awakening the Talents Within by Daryl Green

Dealing with People You Can't Stand by Dr. Rick Brinkman and Dr. Rick Kieshner

Financial Peace by Dave Ramsey

How to Win Friends & Influence People by Dale Carnegie

My Cup Runneth Over: Setting Goals for Single Parents and Working Couples by Daryl Green

Strategic Thinking

Anatomy of a Trend by Henrik Vejlgaard

Growing Your Business Globally by Robert Taft

The Portable MBA in Entrepreneurship by William Bygrave and Andrew Zacharakis

Small Business Enterprises/Home-based Businesses

Four Steps to Building a Profitable Business by Deborah Brown-Volkman

Going Part-time by Cindy Tolliver & Nancy Chambers

How to Start a Home-Based Writing Business by Lucy Parker

The Best Home Business for the 21st Century by Sarah & Paul Edward

WEBSITES FOR JOB STRATEGIES

Smart Business www.smartbiz.com

Working Solo www.workingsolo.com

Entrepreneur www.entrepreneur.com

The Wall Street Journal reporters and columnists have developed a website full of tips for all types of job seekers entitled, "How-To Guide for Careers." These websites are listed below:

Your Career in a Tough Economy
- How to Stand Out From the Competition
- How to Identify Industries That Are Hiring
- How to Make the Most of a Furlough

How to Start a Job Search
- How to Fine-Tune Your Résumé
- How to Write a Résumé
- How to Protect Your Privacy When Job Hunting
- How to Write a Cover Letter
- How to Avoid a Layoff
- How to Find a Career Coach
- How to Find Companies With Flexible Work Arrangements

How to Succeed in a Job Interview
- How to Prepare for a Job Interview
- How to Say Thanks After an Interview
- How to Discuss Career Setbacks in an Interview
- How to Negotiate Salary

Managing Your Career
- How to Get a Raise
- How to Ace a Performance Review
- How to Change Careers
- How to Work From Home
- How to Become Your Own Boss

How to Overcome Career Obstacles
- How to Recover From a Bad Performance Review
- How to Deal With a Bully of a Boss
- How to Handle Office Politics
- How to Quit a Job

How to Identify Job Opportunities
- How to Search for a Job Online
- How to Work a Career Fair
- How to Network Your Way to a Job

How to Work With Executive Recruiters
- How to Work With Executive Recruiters
- What to Say When a Recruiter Calls
- How to Build Relationships With Recruiters
- How to Find Recruiters in Your Niche

Appendix B

TOP 2009 EMPLOYERS FOR ENTRY POSITIONS

Below is a list of 2009 best employers who are dedicated to the development of college graduates and represents a variety of companies:

Rank	Company Name	Industry	Projected Entry Level Hires
1	Verizon Wireless	Telecommunications	13,198
2	Enterprise Rent-A-Car	Automotive Rental, Leasing	8,000
3	Internal Revenue Service	Financial Data Services	5,000
4	Progressive Insurance	Insurance: Property and Casualty (stock)	4,200
5	DDP Holdings	Diversified Financials	4,000
6	Teach For America	Education	4,000
7	AT&T	Telecommunications	3,428
8	Deloitte & Touche USA LLP	Other	3,051
9	Hertz	Automotive Rental, Leasing	3,000
10	Federal Bureau of Investigation	Security and Law Enforcement	2,950
11	KPMG LLP	Other	2,400
12	Boeing	Aerospace and Defense	2,200
13	Lockheed Martin	Aerospace and Defense	2,025
14	Walgreens	General Merchandisers	2,000
15	Northrop Grumman	Aerospace and Defense	1,600
16	City Year	Education	1,500
17	Intel	Electronics, Electrical Equipment	1,500
18	National Security Agency	Security and Law Enforcement	1,500
19	PNC Financial Services Group	Diversified Financials	1,500
20	PricewaterhouseCoopers	Other	1,464
21	Chevron	Energy	1,400
22	Southwest Airlines	Airlines	1,400
23	General Electric	Energy	1,350
24	Wal-Mart Stores, Inc.	General Merchandisers	1,340
25	Sodexo	Diversified Outsourcing Services	1,288
26	Microsoft	Computer Software	1,250
27	Aerotek	Other	1,000
28	C.H. Robinson Worldwide	Transportation and Logistics	1,000
29	Education Management	Education	1,000
30	Fastenal	Building Materials, Glass	1,000
31	Mutual of Omaha	Insurance: Life, Health (mutual)	1,000
32	U.S. Air Force	Aerospace and Defense	1,000
33	U.S. Department of Labor	Other	1,000
34	U.S. Department of State	Other	1,000

35	American Express	Diversified Financials	850
36	Accenture	Diversified Outsourcing Services	800
37	Staples	Computers, Office Equipment	800
38	Target Corporation	General Merchandisers	800
39	AFLAC	Insurance: Life, Health (mutual)	750
40	Capgemini	Information Technology Services	750
41	ExxonMobil	Petroleum Refining	750
42	General Dynamics	Aerospace and Defense	710
43	Kohl's Department Stores	Apparel	700
44	The Sherwin-Williams Company	Other	700
45	EMC Corporation	Computer Peripherals	659
46	Raytheon Company	Aerospace and Defense	651
47	New York Life Insurance Company	Insurance: Life, Health (mutual)	650
48	Northwestern Mutual Financial Network	Diversified Financials	650
49	USDA Forest Service	Other	650
50	BearingPoint	Information Technology Services	600
51	Boy Scouts of America	Other	600
52	Cummins	Other	600
53	Epic Systems	Computer Software	600
54	Fidelity Investments	Diversified Financials	600
55	Procter & Gamble	Other	600
56	U.S. Patent & Trademark Office	Other	600
57	T-Mobile	Telecommunications	590
58	Hewlett Packard	Computers, Office Equipment	548
59	Caterpillar	Industrial and Farm Equipment	500
60	Grant Thornton LLP	Other	500
61	Pacific Park	Entertainment	500
62	Valpak	Advertising, Marketing	500
63	RSM McGladrey	Other	480
64	Travelers	Insurance: Property and Casualty (mutual)	480
65	Fluor	Engineering, Construction	475
66	Mercury Insurance	Insurance: Property and Casualty (stock)	475
67	Merrill Lynch & Company	Diversified Financials	460
68	Cerner	Information Technology Services	450
69	Liberty Mutual	Insurance: Property and Casualty (mutual)	450
70	NAVAIR	Aerospace and Defense	450
71	Pennsylvania Department of Public Welfare	Other	450
72	The Fund for Public Interest Research	Other	450
73	Genentech	Other	420
74	CIGNA	Insurance: Life, Health (stock)	415

75	Naval Acquisition Career Center	Advertising, Marketing	405
76	BAE SYSTEMS	Aerospace and Defense	400
77	RSM McGladrey	Other	400
78	Schlumberger	Oil and Gas Equipment, Services	400
79	The Hartford Financial Services Group	Insurance: Life, Health (mutual)	400
80	Compass Group, North America	Food Services	390
81	The Ad Group	Diversified Outsourcing Services	390
82	Aetna	Insurance: Life, Health (mutual)	375
83	Jos. A. Bank Clothiers	Apparel	350
84	Pearson Education	Publishing, Printing	350
85	Rockwell Collins	Electronics, Electrical Equipment	350
86	Shoney's North America	Food Services	350
87	T. Rowe Price	Diversified Financials	350
88	Naval Sea System Command	Aerospace and Defense	340
89	URS Corporation	Engineering, Construction	325
90	Chrysler LLC	Motor Vehicles and Parts	320
91	Ford Motor Company	Motor Vehicles and Parts	320
92	84 Lumber Company	Building Materials, Glass	300
93	Crotched Mountain	Health Care: Medical Facilities	300
94	Hilti	Engineering, Construction	300
95	Konica Minolta Business Solutions	Computers, Office Equipment	300
96	Philip Morris USA	Other	300
97	Cypress Semiconductor Corporation	Semiconductors and Other Electronic Components	280
98	GEICO	Insurance: Property and Casualty (stock)	275
99	Macy's, Inc.	General Merchandisers	275
100	United States Steel Corporation	Metals	275

Source: http://www.collegegrad.com/topemployers/2009_entry_level.php.

Appendix C

50+ SAVVY STRATEGIES FOR GAINING EMPLOYMENT

01 Know what you desire from your ideal job
02 Keep a positive attitude
03 Visualize your success daily
04 Learn to listen
05 Seek out wise counsel from experience people instead of resisting it
06 Stay in contact with your college career center
07 Network, network, network!!!
08 Develop a 30 second pitch speech for potential job opportunities
09 Determine your value added to an organization if you are hired
10 Check out www.usajobs.com for government vacancies
11 Check out www.chronicle.com for academic vacancies
12 Apply on online employment sites such as Monster, Indeed, and Yahoo! Jobs
13 Be aggressive by applying on at least 100 jobs by the end of the year
14 Cater to things that build character and integrity
15 Invest in activities that bring you closer to your personal goals
16 Write positive affirmations about yourself daily to reassure you of your worth
17 Build a good resume
18 Read two-three books a month to become an expert in a subject
19 Attend a network event
20 Visit a library daily
21 Talk with past employers about any upcoming opportunities
22 Stay alert on social networks such as Twitter, Facebook, and Linkedin
23 Reassess your work experience

24 Practice interviewing skills

25 Network, network, network!!! (repeat!)

26 Stay current on news events

27 Write a daily journal

28 Register and participate with online employment services such as Monster.com

29 Participate in online employment tools on Linkedin

30 Keep a positive attitude

31 Evaluate joining the military in order to gain work experience

32 Join Toastmasters, International to become a better communicator

33 Surround yourself with positive people

34 Meditate daily

35 Present a seminar

36 Volunteer where you can increase your skills in the desired area

37 Be flexible

38 Do extensive research on organizations prior to interviewing

39 Take a short course online

40 Attend career fairs

41 Grow your spiritual self in order to build strength

42 Network with alumni organizations

43 Join a writers group

44 Write an article as an expert

45 Send in a letter to the editor or be a guest columnist

46 Attend industry conferences

47 Act quickly on job leads

48 Get tons of recommendations

49 Talk with past employers about upcoming positions

50 Participate in mock interviews

51 Define, promote, and protect your brand offline and online

52 Pursue your interests

53 Be mobile, flexible, and adaptable

54 Network, network, network!!! (repeat again!)

55 Study abroad to gain international experience

56 Learn a new language

57 Develop a niche or special talent

58 Think critically

59 Grow, stimulate, and promote your creativity

60 Understand corporate culture

Appendix D

2010 BEST PLACES TO LIVE

The following are the 2010 best places to live according to CNN Money.com:

Rank	City	Population
1	Eden Prairie, MN	64,000
2	Columbia/Ellicott City, MD	155,000
3	Newton, MA	82,000
4	Bellevue, WA	124,000
5	McKinney, TX	125,000
6	Fort Collins, CO	141,000
7	Overland Park, KS	175,000
8	Fishers, IN	69,000
9	Ames, IA	60,000
10	Rogers, AR	57,000
11	Plymouth, MN	76,000
12	Highlands Ranch, CO	98,000
13	Woodbury, MN	58,000
14	Carmel, IN	67,000
15	Eagan, MN	64,000
16	Allen, TX	84,000
17	Shawnee, KS	61,000
18	South Jordan, UT	51,000
19	Broomfield, CO	55,000
20	Apple Valley, MN	50,000
21	Missouri City, TX	75,000
22	Irvine, CA	208,000
23	Cary, NC	130,000
24	Rowlett, TX	58,000
25	Gaithersburg, MD	
26	O'Fallon, MO	77,000
27	Lee's Summit, MO	89,000
28	Waltham, MA	60,000
29	Abington, PA	54,000
30	Centreville, VA	54,000
31	Rockville, MD	61,000
32	West Chester, OH	60,000
33	Loveland, CO	66,000
34	Franklin, NJ	61,000
35	Edmond, OK	83,000
36	Gilbert, AZ	216,000
37	Mentor, OH	52,000

38	Yorba Linda, CA	66,000
39	Brookline, MA	58,000
40	Chapel Hill, NC	54,000
41	Clarkstown, NY	83,000
42	Amherst, NY	115,000
43	Bolingbrook, IL	71,000
44	Coral Springs, FL	126,000
45	Orem, UT	94,000
46	Ann Arbor, MI	116,000
47	Alexandria, VA	145,000
48	Coconut Creek, FL	50,000
49	Blue Springs, MO	56,000
50	Waukesha, WI	68,000
51	Rio Rancho, NM	82,000
52	Weymouth, MA	53,000
53	White Plains, NY	57,000
54	Naperville, IL	143,000
55	West Hartford, CT	63,000
56	Mount Prospect, IL	54,000
57	Piscataway, NJ	53,000
58	Arvada, CO	107,000
59	Arlington Heights, IL	73,000
60	St. Peters, MO	56,000
61	West Jordan, UT	95,000
62	Meridian, ID	67,000
63	Pleasanton, CA	67,000
64	Shoreline, WA	54,000
65	Rocklin, CA	53,000
66	Franklin, TN	58,000
67	Stillwater, OK	53,000
68	Iowa City, IA	73,000
69	Eau Claire, WI	66,000
70	Norman, OK	109,000
71	Scottsdale, AZ	235,000
72	Wellington, FL	55,000
73	Wayne, NJ	53,000
74	Bismarck, ND	60,000
75	West Des Moines, IA	55,000
76	Roswell, GA	96,000
77	Sioux Falls, SD	161,000
78	Stamford, CT	119,000
79	Millcreek, PA	54,000
80	St. George, UT	78,000
81	Broken Arrow, OK	93,000
82	New Rochelle, NY	75,000
83	Warwick, RI	84,000
84	Bristol, CT	61,000

85	Chesapeake, VA	220,000
86	Fargo, ND	97,000
87	Hamden, CT	58,000
88	Ramapo, NY	116,000
89	Middletown, NJ	69,000
90	Norwalk, CT	83,000
91	Suffolk, VA	82,000
92	Hillsboro, OR	94,000
93	Owensboro, KY	56,000
94	Nashua, NH	87,000
95	Madison, WI	233,000
96	Appleton, WI	71,000
97	Grand Forks, ND	53,000
98	Beaverton, OR	92,000
99	Idaho Falls, ID	54,000
100	Mount Pleasant, SC	68,000

Appendix E

Government Employement Abroad
Below is a sample of government jobs abroad:
INTERNATIONAL
VACANCY ANNOUNCEMENTS

United Nations and Other International Organizations

August 25 – September 7, 2010

http://www.state.gov/p/io/empl/

Qualified individuals interested in competing for any of the listed vacancies should
submit their applications directly to the international organization of interest.
Organization addresses/contacts are provided on the Department's Internet Site noted above.

WORKING FOR AN INTERNATIONAL ORGANIZATION
HAS MANY BENEFITS
Typical benefits include:

Competitive Salary
Generous Health Benefits Plan
Attractive Pension Plan
Education Grant for Dependents (including college – 4 years)
Generous Leave
Home Leave Travel Costs
Relocation Costs
Holidays (10+)

Most salaries shown are NET of taxes and include a cost-of-living adjustment. Additional allowances & benefits apply.

POSITION TITLE	International Organization (IO)	(Vacancy Number)	Duty Station
(Requirements: Degree; Experience; Foreign Languages)		Grade Net Salary 1/	Closing Date

SENIOR POSTS

1 DEPUTY DIRECTOR (Pblc Governance & Territorial Dev Directorate); Org for Econ Co-Op & Dev (OECD);   (3680);   Paris, France
   (AdvDeg: Econ; 15+ yrs exp; Fr);   A6; $205K Closing date: 08/27/10

2 REPRESENTATIVE TO THE AFRICAN UNION;   Joint UN Program on HIV/AIDS (UNAIDS); (UNAIDS/10/FT42); Addis Ababa, Ethiopia
   (AdvDeg: Int'lRel-Dev/Pol-SocSci/Diplom; 15 yrs (nat'l-int'l) exp; Fr);   D-1; $148K Closing date: 08/27/10

3 PROJ MNGR, LOTFA (Law & Order Trust Fund for Afghanistan) Proj;   UN Development Prog (UNDP);   (18710); Kabul, Afghanistan
   (AdvDeg: Pol-SocSci/Econ; 15 yrs democratic govrnanc exp);   P-6 (D-1); $139K Closing date: 08/28/10

4 DIRECTOR, Procurement Division;   UN Secretariat (UN); (10-ADM-OFC OF CENTRAL SUPPORT SERVICE-15455-R-NEW YORK(G); NY
   (AdvDeg: Bus-PblcAdm/Cmmrce/Engin/Fin/Law; 15+ yrs Logis/supply chain mgmt exp);   D-2; $180K Closing date: 08/28/10

5 SUBREGIONAL COORDINATOR for Central Africa;   Food & Agri Org (FAO);   (OSD/223/10);   Libreville, Gabon
   (AdvDeg: TechAreaRelated toUNMandate; extnsv mgmt & dev issues exp; Fr);   D-1; $159K Closing date: 08/30/10

6 CHIEF OF MISSION;   Int'l Org for Migration (IOM);   (VN 2010/26 (O) – EXT); Islamabad, Pakistan
   (AdvDeg: Pol-SocSci/Int'lRel/BusAdm; 15+ yrs migration & dev exp; Fr/Sp/RegionalLang);   D-1; $136K Closing date: 08/30/10

7 CHIEF INFORMATION OFFICER;   UN Edu, Sci & Cult Org (UNESCO);   (ADM-022);   Paris, France
   (AdvDeg: BehavSci/BusMgmt/Adm/CompSci; 15+ yrs nat'l-int'l exp; Fr);   D-2; $175K Closing date: 08/30/10

8 DIRECTOR, Technical Cooperation Bureau;   Int'l Civil Aviation Org (ICAO);   (PC 2010/15/D-2); Montreal, Canada
   (AdvDeg: AviatTechField with Pblc-BusAdm/DevEcon; 15+ yrs exp);   D-2; $171K Closing date: 08/31/10

9 DIRECTOR, Argentina Operations Center;   UN Ofc for Proj Srvcs (UNOPS); (VA/2010/LCO/AROC/001);   Buenos Aires, Argentina
   (AdvDeg: SocSci/PblcAdm/Int'lRel/BusAdm/OrgDev/Mgt/Mrktng-PR/Engin; 15+ yrs nat'l&int'l exp; Sp); D-1; $131K Closing date: 08/31/10

10 DEPUTY DIRECTOR, Ofc of HRM; UN Secretariat (UN);   (10-ADM-HUMAN RESOURCES MANAGEMENT-15324-R-NEW YORK(G); NY
   (AdvDeg: HRM/Bus-PblcAdm/SocSci; 15+ yrs exp);   D-1; $167K Closing date: 08/31/10

11 EXECUTIVE SECRETARY;   World Health Org (WHO);   (HQ/10/HTM/FT362);   Geneva, Switz
   (AdvDeg: Med/HlthSci/Epidem/CommunicableDiseaseControl; 10 yrs nat'l-int'l exp);   D-1; $186K Closing date: 08/31/10

12 DIRECTOR, Coordination & Response Division;   UN Secretariat (UN);   (10-HRA-OCHA-15319-R-NEW YORK; NY
   (AdvDeg: Int'lLaw/Int'lRel/Econ/SocAdm; 15+ yrs exp);   D-2; $180K Closing date: 09/01/10

13 ASSISTANT DIRECTOR-GENERAL, Technical Coop Dept;   Food & Agriculture Org (FAO);   TC/209/10;   Rome, Italy
   (AdvDeg: Econ/AgriEcon; extnsv exp; Fr/Sp);   ADG; $209K Closing date: 09/06/10

14 CHIEF, Administrative Services/Dept of Peacekp Ops;   UN Secretariat (UN); (10-ADM-PMSS-424707-R-MULTIPLE D/S); Multiple D/S
   (AdvDeg: Bus-PblcAdm/HRM/Fin/Acct/Law; 15+ yrs exp; Fr);   D-1; $TBD Closing date: 09/05/10

15 HEAD, Subreg Ofc for S&SW Asia;   UN Econ&SocComm Asia&Pacific; (10-ADM-escap sasswa-15592-R-NEW DELHI (G)); New Delhi, India
   (AdvDeg: Econ/SocSci; 15+ yrs (incl int'l) exp);   D-1; $141K Closing date: 09/05/10

16 DEPUTY CONTROLLER, Financial & Adm Mgmt Div;   UN High Commissioner for Refugees (UNHCR);   (10001687); Geneva, Switz
   (AdvDeg: Fin/BusAdm/Acct & CPA-CA; 20 yrs (10+ yrs int'l) exp);   D-1; $186K Closing date: 09/07/10

17 CHIEF OF STAFF;   UN Ofc to the African Union (UNOAU);   (10-POL-UNOAU-424734-R-ADDIS ABABA); Ethiopia
   (AdvDeg: Int'lRel/PolSci/Bus-PblcAdm/Mgmt/Law/MilitaryStdys; 15+ yrs exp);   D-2; $159K Closing date: 09/10/10

18 CHIEF OF MISSION SUPPORT/Dept of Peacekp Ops;   UN Secretariat (UN); (10-ADM-PMSS-424740-R-MULTIPLE D/S);
Multiple D/S
  (AdvDeg: Bus-PblcAdm/Fin/Acct/Law; 15+ yrs exp);   D-1; $TBD Closing date: 09/11/10

19 SECRETARY-GENERAL OF THE INTERNATIONAL TRANSPORT FORUM; Org for Econ Co-Op & Dev (OECD);   (3704);
Paris, France
  (AdvDeg: Transport/Econ/Bsns; 15+ yrs exp);   A7; $224K Closing date: 09/20/10

20 CHIEF OF BRANCH (Africa);   UN Secretariat (UN);   (10-HR1-OHCHR-15690-R-GENEVA);   Switz
  (AdvDeg: Law/HumanRts/PolSci/Int'lRel; 15+ yrs (10+ yrs int'l-lvl human rts) exp; Fr);   D-1; $186K Closing date:
09/12/10

21 SENIOR ADVISER, Policy & Advocacy;   World Health Org (WHO);   (UNITAID/10/FT390);   Geneva, Switz
  (AdvDeg: PblcPol/PolSci/Int'lRel/Law; 10 yrs (5 yrs int'l) exp; Fr);   (P-6)D-1; $186K Closing date: 09/17/10

22 CHIEF PUBLIC INFORMATION OFCR/Dept of Peacekp Ops; UN Secretariat (UN); (10-PUB-PMSS-424685-R-MULTIPLE D/S);
Multiple D/S
  (AdvDeg: StratCommun/Commun/PblcRel/Int'lRel/Broadcst/SocSci/BusAdm/Mgmt; 15+ yrs exp; Fr);   D-1; $TBD Closing date:
09/27/10

23 CHIEF LIBRARIAN;   UN Ofc at Geneva (UNOG);   (10-ADM-UN OFFICE AT GENEVA-16264-R-GENEVA);
Switz
  (Deg: PolSci/Int'lRel/Law/Econ/SocSci/AdvDeg Libr-InfoSci/Archives (RcrdsMgmt); 15+ yrs exp; Fr);   D-1; $186K Closing date:
09/29/10

24 DIRECTOR (Family & Community Health);   World Health Org (WHO);   (HQ/10/FCH/FT402);   Geneva, Switz
  (AdvDeg: Nursing/Midwifery/SocSci/Hlth; 10 yrs (3 yrs int'l) exp);   D-1; $186K Closing date: 09/29/10

25 CHIEF INFORMATION OFFICER / DIRECTOR, CIO Division;   Food & Agriculture Org (FAO);   (CIO/225/10);
Rome, Italy
  (AdvDeg: CompSci/Engin/BusAdm; extnsv IT exp; UN Lang);   D-2; $170K Closing date: 09/30/10

26 DIRECTOR, UNRWA Operations, Jordan;   UN Relief & Works Agency (UNRWA);   (10-FO-JO-63);   Amman,
Jordan
  (AdvDeg: PolSci/SocSci/Pblc-BusAdm/Int'lRel; 15+ yrs (10+ yrs gov't-int'l org/5 yrs sr-lvl) exp);   D-1; $143K Closing date:
09/30/10

27 CHIEF OF OFC, Ofc of Under-Sec-Gen; UN Secretariat (UN); (10-ADM-DEPT FOR GA & CONFERENCE MGMT-15727-R-NEW
YORK); NY
  (AdvDeg: Int'lRel/Econ/SocSci; 15+ yrs conf servicing exp);   D-1; $167K Closing date: 10/02/10

28 DIRECTOR, UNICRI;   UN Interregional Crime & Justice Rsrch Instit (UNICRI);   (10-ADM-UNOV UNICRI-16217-R-
TURIN (E));   Italy
  (AdvDeg: Int'lRel/Econ/SocSci; 15+ yrs conf servicing exp);   D-1; $167K Closing date: 10/02/10

29 DIR, Sub-Reg Ofc for the Carib; Econ Comm for LatinAm & Carib (ECLAC); (10-ADM-ECLAC-15488-R-PORT OF SPAIN(G));
Trin&Tobago
  (AdvDeg: Econ/SocSci; 15+ yrs (incl Caribbean region) exp; Sp);   D-1; $149K Closing date: 10/08/10

30 DIRECTOR, NatRsrces & Infrastructure Div; Econ Comm for LatinAm & Carib (ECLAC); (10-ADM-ECLAC-15489-R-
SANTIAGO(G));   Chile
  (AdvDeg: Econ/Engin/NatRsrcesMgmt/PblcUtilitiesMgmt; 15+ yrs exp; Sp);   D-1; $143K Closing date:
10/08/10

31 CHIEF FINANCIAL OFFICER;   UN Edu, Sci & Cult Org (UNESCO);   (BOC-030);   Paris, France
  (AdvDeg: Mgmt/Fin/Acct; 15 yrs exp);   D-2; $175K Closing date: 10/10/10

32 EXECUTIVE SECRETARY;   UN Environment Program (UNEP); (10-ADM-UN ENVIRONMENT PROGRAM-15731-R-
GENEVA);   Switz
  (AdvDeg: Law/PolSci/NatSci/Chem/Econ/PblcAdm; 15+ yrs (incl envir field int'l org) exp);   D-2; $201K Closing date:
10/12/10

PROFESSIONAL POSTS

33 HUMAN RESOURCES OFFICER;   International Fund for Agricultural Development (IFAD);   (10/21/P);   Rome,
Italy
  (Deg: RsrceMgmt/OrgDev/BusAdmin/Law/Econ; 5 yrs exp);   P-3; $91K Closing date: 08/26/10

34 FINANCE SPECIALIST, Assistant Treasurer;   Pan American Health Org (PAHO); (PAHO/10/FT354);   WashDC
  (Deg: Acct/Fin/BusAdmin; 7 yrs nat'l-int'l exp; Sp);   P-3; $84K Closing date: 08/26/10

35 WOMEN, PEACE, & GOVERNANCE UNIT MANAGER;   UN Development Fund for Women (UNIFEM); (18475);   Kabul,
Afghanistan
  (AdvDeg: Govern/Int'lDev/PblcPol/SocSci; 5 yrs exp);   P-3; $81K Closing date: 08/26/10

36 ASSOCIATE PROGRAM OFFICER; UN Framework Convention on Climate Change (UNFCCC);   (VA 10/066/SDM);   Bonn,

Germany
  (Deg: EnvirSci/PblcAdm/Law/PblcFin; 3+ yrs climate chng/pblic adm/dev mgmt exp);   P-2; $73K Closing date:
08/26/10

37 SECTION HEAD, Prog Support & Coordination Div;   Int'l Atomic Energy Agency (IAEA);   (2010/060);   Vienna,
Austria
  (AdvDeg: Humanities/SocSci/Mgmt/Bus-PblcAdm/Econ; 10+ yrs (3 yrs int'l) exp);   P-5; $135K Closing date:
08/27/10

38 ADVISER, Determinants of Health;   Pan American Health Org (PAHO); (PAHO/10/FT357);   WashDC
  (AdvDeg: PblcHlth; 9 yrs nat'l-int'l exp; Sp);   P-4; $101K Closing date: 08/27/10

39 SENIOR SPECIALIST;   Science & Technology Ctr in Ukraine (STCU);   (##2010/-02);   Kyiv, Ukraine
  (Deg: ProjMgmt; proj mgmt capacity incl process dev & execution exp);   N/A; $TBD Closing date: 08/27/10

40 PROCUREMENT OFFICER/Dept of Peacekp Ops;   UN Secretariat (UN); (10-PRO-PMSS-424577-R-MULTIPLE D/S);
Multiple D/S
  (AdvDeg: Bus-PblcAdm/Cmmrce/Engin/Law; 5+ yrs exp);   P-3; $TBD Closing date: 08/28/10

41 PROCUREMENT OFFICER/Dept of Peacekp Ops;   UN Secretariat (UN); (10-PRO-PMSS-424579-R-MULTIPLE D/S);
Multiple D/S
  (AdvDeg: Bus-PblcAdm/Cmmrce/Engin/Law; 7+ yrs exp);   P-4; $TBD Closing date: 08/28/10

42 CHIEF PROCUREMENT OFFICER/Dept of Peacekp Ops; UN Secretariat (UN); (10-PRO-PMSS-424581-R-MULTIPLE D/S);
Multiple D/S
  (AdvDeg: Bus-PblcAdm/Cmmrce/Engin/Law; 7+ yrs (3+ yrs suprvsry exp);   P-4; $TBD Closing date: 08/28/10

43 PROGRAM BUDGET OFFICER;   UN Secretariat (UN);   (10-ADM-OPPBA-15424-R-NEW YORK);   NY
  (AdvDeg: BusAdm/Fin/PblcAdm; 7+ yrs exp);   P-4; $116K Closing date: 08/28/10

44 SENIOR SAFETY OFFICER;   Org for Prohibition of CW (OPCW);   (E-DDG/HSB/SSO/FO018/P-5/34/06-10);   The
Hague, NL
  (Deg: SciDiscip (Chem/OccupHygiene/Hlth & Safety/NBC Defense); 15+ yrs CW safety exp; Dutch);   P-5; $127K Closing date:
08/29/10

45 SAFETY OFFICER;   Org for Prohibition of CW (OPCW);   (E-DDG/HSB/SO/FO020/P-3/35/06-10);   The
Hague, NL
  (Deg: SciDiscip (NBC Defense/Chem/OccupHygiene/Hlth & Safety); 7+ yrs CW safety/hlth exp; Dutch); P-3; $87K Closing date:
08/29/10

46 PUBLIC INFORMATION OFCR (Radio Mgmt Adviser); UN Secretariat (UN); (10-PUB-UNIPSIL-424686-R-FREETOWN);
Sierra Leone
  (AdvDeg: DevCommun/MediaStdys/Journ/PblcRel; 7+ yrs media dev (5+ yrs sr mgmt) exp; Fr);   P-4; $104K Closing date:
08/29/10

47 FISHERY INFORMATION OFFICER;   Food & Agriculture Org (FAO);   (2441-FIP);   Rome, Italy
  (Deg: Biology (AquaticSci); 5 yrs exp; Fr/Sp);   P-3; $91K Closing date: 08/30/10

48 REGIONAL OFFICER, Flight Safety;   Int'l Civil Aviation Org (ICAO);   (PC 2010/28/P-4);   Bangkok,
Thailand
  (AdvDeg: AeronautEngin/Aviat-RelatedTechDiscip; 10 yrs exp);   P-4; $100K Closing date: 08/30/10

49 ADVISER, Chronic Diseases;   Pan American Health Org (PAHO); (PAHO/10/FT358);   Mexico City, Mexico
  (AdvDeg: PblcHlth; 9 yrs nat'l-int'l exp; Sp);   P-4; $98K Closing date: 08/30/10

50 ADVISER, Health Technologies Management;   Pan American Health Org (PAHO);   (PAHO/10/FT360);   WashDC
  (AdvDeg: PblcHlth; 9 yrs nat'l-int'l exp; Sp);   P-4; $101K Closing date: 08/30/10

51 CONFERENCE SERVICES OFCR;   UN Secretariat (UN); (10-ADM-DEPT FOR GA & CONFERENCE MGMT-15478-R-NEW
YORK); NY
  (AdvDeg: BusAdm/Mgmt; 5+ yrs exp);   P-3; $96K Closing date: 08/30/10

52 CENTER HEAD (Incident & Emergency);   Int'l Atomic Energy Agency (IAEA);   (2010/006);   Vienna, Austria
  (AdvDeg: NuclField; 10+ yrs nucl safety-radiation protection exp);   P-5; $135K Closing date: 08/31/10

53 PROGRAM OFFICER, Conservation Planning;   Int'l Union for Conservation of Nature (IUCN);   (193);   Cambridge,
UK
  (AdvDeg: Ecology/Biology/Geography; 5+ yrs biodiversity exp; Fr/Sp);   P-1; $72K Closing date: 08/31/10

54 ECONOMIST/POLICY ANALYST;   Org for Econ Co-Op & Dev (OECD);   (3687);   Paris, France
  (AdvDeg: Econ; 3+ yrs exp);   A2/A3; $104K Closing date: 08/31/10

55 INFLUENZA SURVEILLANCE SPECIALIST;   Secretariat of the Pacific Community (SPC); (10/47); Noumea, New
Caledonia
  (AdvDeg: PblcHlth/Epidemiol; extnsv dev cntry exp);   N/A; $TBD Closing date: 08/31/10

56 HEAD, Donor Development;   United Nations Children's Fund (UNICEF);   (N/A);   London, UK
  (AdvDeg: BusAdmin/Fin/Acct/Int'lDev; 5+ yrs fundraising exp);   N/A; $TBD Closing date: 08/31/10

57 ASSOCIATE LEGAL OFFICER;   UN Secretariat (UN);   (10-LEG-UNS-15815-R-THE HAGUE);   NL
(AdvDeg: Law (Int'l/Crim/HumanitLaw); 2+ yrs nat'l-int'l exp);   P-2; $72K Closing date: 08/31/10

58 INFORMATION & COMMUNICATIONS TECHNOLOGY OFFICER;   Food & Agriculture Org (FAO);   (2442-CIO);
Cairo, Egypt
(Deg: CompSci/Engin/Math; 7 yrs exp; Arabic/Fr);   P-4; $97K Closing date: 09/01/10

59 INFORMATION & COMMUNICATIONS TECHNOLOGY OFFICER;   Food & Agriculture Org (FAO);   (2443-CIO);
Budapest, Hungary
(Deg: CompSci/Engin/Math; 7 yrs exp; Rus/Fr);   P-4; $97K Closing date: 09/01/10

60 WASTE SAFETY SPECIALIST;   Int'l Atomic Energy Agency (IAEA);   (2010/067);   Vienna, Austria
(AdvDeg: Nucl-Physical Sci/Engin; 7+ yrs exp);   P-4; $111K Closing date: 09/01/10

61 PLANT BREEDER/GENETICIST;   Int'l Atomic Energy Agency (IAEA);   (2010/079);   Vienna, Austria
(AdvDeg: PlantBreed/Genetcs (MutationTechnqs/PlantBiotechnol); 7+ yrs mutatn breed/dev cntry exp); P-4; $111K Closing date:
09/01/10

62 LABORATORY HEAD;   Int'l Atomic Energy Agency (IAEA);   (2010/080);   Vienna, Austria
(AdvDeg: PlantBreeding/Genetics; 10+ yrs nat'l & int'l exp);   P-5; $135K Closing date: 09/01/10

63 ANALYTICAL CHEMIST;   Int'l Atomic Energy Agency (IAEA);   (2010/081);   Vienna, Austria
(Deg: Analyt-OrganicChem; 2 yrs exp);   P-2; $77K Closing date: 09/01/10

64 PARTNERSHIPS ADVISER;   UN Population Fund (UNFPA);   (1637); Johannesburg, S. Africa
(AdvDeg: PblcHlth/Med/Sociol/Demog/Gender/Int'lRel-Dev/Econ/PblcAdm; 10 yrs exp);   ICS-12 (=P5); $114K Closing date:
09/01/10

65 TECHNICAL ADVISER – Repro Hlth/Maternal Health;   UN Population Fund (UNFPA);   (1638);   Dakar,
Senegal
(AdvDeg: PblcHlth/Med/Sociol/HlthSys/Econ; 10 yrs (7 yrs int'l) exp);   ICS-12 (=P5); $124K Closing date:
09/01/10

66 SOCIAL AFF OFCR (Youth Employmnt & Empwrmnt Spec); UN Secretariat (UN); (10-SOC-UNIPSIL-424671-R-FREETOWN);
Sierra Leone
(AdvDeg: SocSci/PolSci/DevStdys/Int'lAff; 7+ yrs exp);   P-4; $104K Closing date: 09/01/10

67 FIELD FINANCE OFFICER;   UN Relief & Works Agency (UNRWA);   (10-FO-GA-62);   Gaza
(AdvDeg: Fin/Acct/BusAdm; 8 yrs exp);   P-4; $105K Closing date: 09/02/10

68 CHIEF SECURITY OFFICER;   UN Interim Force in Lebanon (UNIFIL);   (10-SEC-UNIFIL-424777-R-BEIRUT);
Lebanon
(AdvDeg: BusAdm/Pol-SocSci/Psychol/Int'lRel; 10+ yrs (2+ yrs int'l) exp; Fr/LocalLang);   P-5; $126K Closing date:
09/02/10

69 HUMAN RESOURCES OFFICER (Legal Matters);   Food & Agriculture Org (FAO);   (IRC2013);   Rome, Italy
(Deg: Law; 7 yrs employment law-employee grievances & litigations exp; Fr/Sp);   P-4; $110K Closing date: 09/03/10

70 ENVIRONMENT OFFICER;   Food & Agriculture Org (FAO);   (CP-020-TCI);   Rome, Italy
(AdvDeg: Geog/NatRsrcesMgmt/EnvirSci/EnvirEngin; 7 yrs (incl dev cntry) exp; Sp);   P-4; $110K Closing date:
09/03/10

71 SENIOR ADVISER TO THE DIRECTOR;   International Labor Organization (ILO);   (RAPS/2/2010/ILO/AIDS/01);
Geneva, Switz
(AdvDeg: PblcHlth/Occ-IndHlth; 10 yrs (7 yrs int'l) exp; Fr/Sp);   P-5; $157K Closing date: 09/03/10

72 SR ECONOMIST (Quantitative Anal of Soc Impact of Globalization);   Int'l Labor Org (ILO);   (RAPS/2/2010/INST/01);
Geneva, Switz
(AdvDeg: Econ; 10+ yrs (7 yrs int'l) exp; Fr/Sp);   P-5; $157K Closing date: 09/03/10

73 SENIOR RELATIONS SPECIALIST (Unit Head);   International Labor Organization (ILO);   (RAPS/2/2010/RELOFF/01);
Geneva, Switz
(AdvDeg: Lit/ModLang/PolSci/Int'lPblcLaw; 10 yrs (7 yrs int'l) exp; Fr&Sp);   P-5; $157K Closing date:
09/03/10

74 COORDINATOR, Occptn Safety, Policy & Mgmt Sys;   International Labor Organization (ILO); (RAPS/2/2010/SAFEWORK/01);
Geneva, Switz
(AdvDeg: OccSafety&Hlth/IndHygiene/Engin/Med; 10+ yrs (7 yrs int'l) exp; Fr/Sp);   P-5; $157K Closing date:
09/03/10

75 DEPUTY DIRECTOR;   International Labor Organization (ILO);   (RAPS/2/2010/AS/02);   New Delhi,
India
(AdvDeg: Mgmt/BusMgmt; 10 yrs (7 yrs int'l) exp; Fr/Sp);   P-5; $119K Closing date: 09/03/10

76 HEAD OF PRTNRSHP, Rsrce Mobilization & UN Reform Unit;   Int'l Labor Organization (ILO);   (RAPS/2/2010/AS/03);
Bangkok, Thailand
(AdvDeg: Econ/SocSci/Law/Int'lStdys; 10+ yrs (7 yrs int'l) exp; Fr/Sp);   P-5; $121K Closing date: 09/03/10

77 COORDINATOR, Helpdesk for Business;　　International Labor Organization (ILO);　(RAPS/2/2010/EMP MULTI/01);
Geneva, Switz
　(AdvDeg: Law/Mgmt; 10+ yrs (7 yrs int'l) exp; Fr/Sp);　　　　　　　P-5; $157K Closing date: 09/03/10

78 SENIOR ECONOMIST;　　　　　International Labor Organization (ILO);　(RAPS/2/2010/EMP/ELM/01);　　Geneva,
Switz
　(AdvDeg: Econ; 10+ yrs (7 yrs int'l) exp; Fr/Sp);　　　　　　　　P-5; $157K Closing date: 09/03/10

79 COORDINATOR, Green Jobs Program;　International Labor Organization (ILO); (RAPS/2/2010/EMP/ENTERPRISE/01);
Geneva, Switz
　(AdvDeg: Econ/BsnsMgmt/NatRsrce/EnvirMgmt; 10+ yrs (7 yrs int'l) exp; Fr/Sp);　　　P-5; $157K Closing date:
09/03/10

80 PROGRAM MANAGER;　　　　International Labor Organization (ILO);　(RAPS/2/2010/EMP/SEED/01);　　Geneva,
Switz
　(AdvDeg: Econ/Bsns; 10+ yrs (7 yrs int'l) exp; Fr/Sp);　　　　　　P-5; $157K Closing date: 09/03/10

81 REGIONAL SPECIALIST, Social Security;　International Labor Organization (ILO);　　(RAPS/2/2010/AR/01);　Beirut,
Lebanon
　(AdvDeg: Econ/Soc-Int'lSci/PblcAdmin; 10+ yrs (7 yrs int'l) exp);　　　　P-5; $126K Closing date: 09/03/10

82 PROCUREMENT OFCR (Police Sys Dev);　UN Integrated Mission in Timor Leste (UNMIT);　(10-PRO-UNMIT-424615-R-DILI);
Timor Leste
　(AdvDeg: Purchasing-Procuremnt/Bus-PblcAdm/Cmmrce/Law; 5+ yrs exp);　　　　P-3; $87K Closing date: 09/03/10

83 MONITORING & EVALUATION OFCR;　UN Integrated Mission in Timor Leste (UNMIT);　(10-PGM-UNMIT-424617-R-DILI);
Timor Leste
　(AdvDeg: SocSci/PolSci/Law; 5+ yrs (incl dev cntry field) exp);　　　　　P-3; $87K Closing date: 09/03/10

84 COORD OFCR (Donor Liaison&Rsrce Mobiliz);　UN Integrated Mission Timor Leste (UNMIT);　(10-PGM-UNMIT-424613-R-DILI);
Timor Leste
　(AdvDeg: Pol-SocSci/Int'lStdys/BusAdm/Mgmt; 7+ yrs exp);　　　　　　P-4; $105K Closing date: 09/03/10

85 ADMINISTRATIVE / GENERAL SERVICES OFFICER;　UN Secretariat (UN);　(10-ADM-ICTR KIGALI AS-15718-R-KIGALI(G));
Rwanda
　(AdvDeg: Bus-PblcAdm/Logis; 5+ yrs exp; Fr);　　　　　　　　　P-3; $86K Closing date: 09/03/10

86 HUMAN RIGHTS OFFICER;　　　　　UN Secretariat (UN);　　(10-HRI-OHCHR-15772-R-GENEVA);　　Switz
　(AdvDeg: Law/PolSci/Int'lRel; 7+ yrs exp);　　　　　　　　P-4; $130K Closing date: 09/03/10

87 HUMAN RESOURCES OFCR;　UN Econ&SocComm Asia&Pacific (ESCAP);　(10-ADM-ESCAP ASD HRMS-15636-R-
BANGKOK); Thailand
　(AdvDeg: HRM/Bus-PblcAdm/SocSci/Edu; 5+ yrs exp);　　　　　　P-3; $83K Closing date: 09/04/10

88 ASSOCIATE PROGRAM OFFICER;　UN Framework Convention on Climate Change (UNFCCC);　(VA 10/067/CAS);　Bonn,
Germany
　(Deg: Econ/BusAdm/SocSci; 3+ yrs exp);　　　　　　　　　P-2; $73K Closing date: 09/04/10

89 EXPERT (Training);　UN Ofc on Drugs & Crime (UNODC);　(10-ADM-UN OFFICE ON DRUGS AND CRIME-15997-R-KABUL);
Afghanistan
　(AdvDeg: Int'lLaw/CrimLaw/Int'lRel/PolSci/Mgmt-BusStdys; 7+ yrs law enfrcemnt exp);　　P-4; $97K Closing date:
09/04/10

90 SENIOR HUMAN ESOURCES OFCR;　UN Ofc on Drugs & Crime (UNODC);　(10-HRE-UN OFFICE AT GENEVA-15888-
GENEVA);　Switz
　(AdvDeg: Pblc-BusAdm/HRM/Law; 10+ yrs exp; Fr);　　　　　　P-5; $157K Closing date: 09/04/10

91 FINANCE ASSOCIATE;　　　　　Int'l Atomic Energy Agency (IAEA);　　(2010/086);　　Vienna, Austria
　(AdvDeg: Fin/Math/Stats; 2+ yrs exp);　　　　　　　P-2; $77K Closing date: 09/05/10

92 HEAD OF DESIGN, Nahr El-Bared Camp;　UN Relief & Works Agency (UNRWA);　(10-FO-LB-59);　North Lebanon
Area
　(AdvDeg: Arch; 6+ yrs (3 yrs suprvsry) exp);　　　　　　　P-3; $86K Closing date: 09/05/10

93 SR LEGAL AFFAIRS OFFICER / Dept of Peacekp Ops;　UN Secretariat (UN);　(10-LEG-PMSS-424698-R-MULTIPLE D/S);
Multiple D/S
　(AdvDeg: Law (Int'l-Adm-Cmmrcl/CrimLaw); 10+ yrs exp; Fr/LocalLang);　　　　P-5; $TBD Closing date: 09/05/10

94 LEGAL AFFAIRS OFFICER / Dept of Peacekp Ops;　　UN Secretariat (UN);　(10-LEG-PMSS-424696-R-MULTIPLE D/S);
Multiple D/S
　(AdvDeg: Law (Int'l-Adm-Cmmrcl/CrimLaw); 7+ yrs exp; Fr/LocalLang);　　　　P-4; $TBD Closing date: 09/05/10

95 LEGAL OFFICER / Dept of Peacekp Ops;　　UN Secretariat (UN);　(10-LEG-PMSS-424694-R-MULTIPLE D/S);　Multiple
D/S
　(AdvDeg: Law (Int'l-Adm-Cmmrcl/CrimLaw); 5+ yrs exp; Fr/LocalLang);　　　　P-3; $TBD Closing date: 09/05/10

96 SR HUMAN RIGHTS OFFICER / Dept of Peacekp Ops;   UN Secretariat (UN); (10-HRI-PMSS-424692-R-MULTIPLE D/S);
Multiple D/S
  (AdvDeg: Law/PolSci/Int'lRel; 10+ yrs nat'l-int'l exp; Fr/LocalLang);   P-5; $TBD Closing date: 09/05/10

97 HUMAN RIGHTS OFFICER / Dept of Peacekp Ops;   UN Secretariat (UN);   (10-HRI-PMSS-424690-R-MULTIPLE D/S);
Multiple D/S
  (AdvDeg: Law/PolSci/Int'lRel; 7+ yrs nat'l-int'l exp; Fr/LocalLang);   P-4; $TBD Closing date: 09/05/10

98 ADMINISTRATIVE OFFICER;   UN Secretariat (UN);   (10-ADM-DEPARTMENT OF MANAGEMENT-15906-R-NEW
YORK);   NY
  (AdvDeg: Bus-PblcAdm/HR/Fin; 5+ yrs exp);   P-3; $96K Closing date: 09/05/10

99 STATISTICIAN;   Food & Agriculture Org (FAO);   (2445-RLC);   Santiago, Chile
  (AdvDeg: Stats/Econ; 7 yrs agri stats (incl field) exp; Sp);   P-4; $100K Closing date: 09/06/10

100 LIBRARIAN;   Int'l Atomic Energy Agency (IAEA);   (2010/082);   Vienna, Austria
  (Deg: Libr-InfoSci; 5+ yrs; Ger);   P-3; $93K Closing date: 09/06/10

101 NUCLEAR ENGINEER (INPRO);   Int'l Atomic Energy Agency (IAEA);   (2010/085);   Vienna,
Austria
  (AdvDeg: NuclEngin; 7 yrs (5+ yrs int'l) exp);   P-4; $111K Closing date: 09/06/10

102 GRANTS PORTFOLIO ADVISER;   International Fund for Agricultural Development (IFAD);   (10/22/P);
Rome, Italy
  (Deg: BusAdm/Econ/AgriEcon; 5+ yrs exp);   P-3; $91K Closing date: 09/06/10

103 PROCUREMENT OFFICER;   UN Int'l Computing Center (UNICC);   (ICC/10/GVA/493);   Geneva,
Switz
  (AdvDeg: Bus-PblcAdm/Fin; 7 yrs exp; Fr);   P-4; $130K Closing date: 09/06/10

104 ASSOC AVIATION SAFETY OFCR/Dept of Peacekp Ops; UN Secretariat (UN); (10-LOG-PMSS-424555-R-MULTIPLE D/S);
Multiple D/S
  (AdvDeg: AirTrnsprt/AviatEngin/SafetyMgmt/AirTrafficCntrl; 2+ yrs exp; UN lang);   P-2; $TBD Closing date:
09/06/10

105 AVIATION SAFETY OFFICER/Dept of Peacekp Ops;   UN Secretariat (UN); (10-LOG-PMSS-424557-R-MULTIPLE D/S);
Multiple D/S
  (AdvDeg: AirTrnsprt/AviatEngin/SafetyMgmt/BusAdm/AirTrafficCntrl; 5+ yrs exp; UN lang);   P-3; $TBD Closing date:
09/06/10

106 CHIEF AVIATION SAFETY OFFICER/Dept of Peacekp Ops; UN Secretariat (UN); (10-LOG-PMSS-424559-R-MULTIPLE D/S);
Multiple D/S
  (AdvDeg: AirTrnsprt/AviatEngin/SafetyMgmt/BusAdm/AirTrafficCntrl; 7+ yrs exp; UN lang);   P-4; $TBD Closing date:
09/06/10

107 ASSOC AIR OPERATIONS OFCR/Dept of Peacekp Ops;   UN Secretariat (UN); (10-LOG-PMSS-424569-R-MULTIPLE D/S);
Multiple D/S
  (AdvDeg: AirTrnsprt/AeronautEngin/SafetyMgmt/AirTrafficCntrl; 2+ yrs exp; UN lang);   P-2; $TBD Closing date:
09/06/10

108 AIR OPERATIONS OFFICER/Dept of Peacekp Ops;   UN Secretariat (UN); (10-LOG-PMSS-424571-R-MULTIPLE D/S);
Multiple D/S
  (AdvDeg: AviatMgt/Aerospace-AeronautEngin/AirTrnsprtMgt/AirTrafficCntrl; 5+yrs (2+yrs int'l) exp; UN); P-3; $TBD Closing
date: 09/06/10

109 CHIEF AIR OPERATIONS OFFICER/Dept of Peacekp Ops; UN Secretariat (UN); (10-LOG-PMSS-424573-R-MULTIPLE D/S);
Multiple D/S
  (AdvDeg: AviatMgt/Aerospace-AeronautEngin/BusAdm/AirTrafficCntrl; 7+yrs (2+yrs int'l) exp; UN);   P-4; $TBD Closing date:
09/06/10

110 CHIEF AVIATION OFFICER/Dept of Peacekp Ops;   UN Secretariat (UN); (10-LOG-PMSS-424575-R-MULTIPLE D/S);
Multiple D/S
  (AdvDeg: BusAdm/AirTrnsprt/AviatMgmt/AeronautEngin; 10+yrs (3+yrs int'l) exp; UN);   P-5; $TBD Closing date:
09/06/10

111 SENIOR HUMAN RIGHTS ADVISER;   UN Secretariat (UN);   (10-HRI-OHCHR-15576-R-ANTANANARIVO);
Madagascar
  (AdvDeg: HumanRts/Pblc-Int'lLaw/PolSci/Int'lRel; 10+ yrs nat'l-int'l exp; Fr);   P-5; $114K Closing date:
09/06/10

112 HUMAN RIGHTS ADVISER;   UN Secretariat (UN);   (10-HRI-OHCHR-15510-R-GENEVA);
Switz
  (AdvDeg: Law/PolSci/Int'lRel; 5+ yrs nat'l-int'l exp; Fr);   P-3; $108K Closing date: 09/06/10

113 ASSOCIATE BUDGET OFFICER;   UN Framework Convention on Climate Change (UNFCCC);   (VA 10/068/AS);   Bonn,
Germany
  (Deg: BusAdm/SocSci; 3+ yrs exp);   P-2; $73K Closing date: 09/07/10

114 FIELD SAFETY ADVISER; UN High Commissioner for Refugees (UNHCR); (10002122); Geneva, Switz
(Deg: Int'lRel/Law; 8 yrs nat'l-int'l exp; Fr); P-3; $108K Closing date: 09/07/10

115 SR LIAISON & FOOD SECURITY OFFICER; UN High Commissioner for Refugees (UNHCR); (10002187); Geneva, Switz
(AdvDeg: PblcHlth/Nutri/Dev/Econ; 10+ yrs exp; Fr); P-4; $130K Closing date: 09/07/10

116 DEPUTY HEAD OF SERVICE (Resources Mgmt); UN High Commissioner for Refugees (UNHCR); (100012998); Geneva, Switz
(Deg: BusAdm/Econ/Mgmt/Fin-Cmmrce; 17 yrs (10+ yrs int'l) exp; Fr/UN Lang); P-5; $157K Closing date: 09/07/10

117 REGISTRATION OFFICER; UN High Commissioner for Refugees (UNHCR); (10009975); N'Djamena, Chad
(Deg: SocSci/SocWrk/IT; 8 yrs (5 yrs int'l) exp; Fr); P-3; $94K Closing date: 09/07/10

118 HUMAN RIGHTS OFFICER; UN Secretariat (UN); (10-HRI-OHCHR-16145-R-CONAKRY); Guinea
(AdvDeg: Law/PolSci/Int'lRel; 7+ yrs nat'l-int'l exp; Fr); P-4; $97K Closing date: 09/07/10

119 INFORMATION SYSTEMS OFCR (Inspira Support Center); UN Secretariat (UN); (10-IST-DM OHRM ISC-15702-R-BANGKOK); Thailand
(AdvDeg: CompSci/Engin; 5+ yrs PeopleSoft exp); P-3; $83K Closing date: 09/07/10

120 PROG SPECIALST, Regional Sci Bureau/Asia & Pacific; UN Edu, Sci & Cult Org (UNESCO); (AS/RP/INS/SC/0010); Jakarta, Indonesia
(AdvDeg: Biology/Chem/Math/Physics; 7+ yrs exp); P-4; $104K Closing date: 09/08/10

121 FINANCE OFFICER, Bureau of the Comptroller; UN Edu, Sci & Cult Org (UNESCO); (BOC-079); Paris, France
(AdvDeg: Fin/Acct/CPA; 4+ yrs (3 yrs int'l) ERP exp; Fr); P-3; $94K Closing date: 09/08/10

122 LEARNING & TRAINING SPECIALIST; UN Population Fund (UNFPA); (1639); New York, NY
(AdvDeg: HRM/Bus/AdultEdu/SocSci; 7 yrs (incl int'l) exp; Fr/Sp); ICS-11 (P-4); $116K Closing date: 09/08/10

123 TECHNICAL SPECIALIST – Maternal Health; UN Population Fund (UNFPA); (1640); Bamako, Mali
(AdvDeg: PblcHlth; 7 yrs exp; Fr); ICS-11 (P-4); $108K Closing date: 09/08/10

124 HUMAN RESOURCES POLICY OFFICER; UN Relief & Works Agency (UNRWA); (10-HQ-AM-64); Amman, Jordan
(AdvDeg: HRM/Pblc-BusAdm/Law; 8+ yrs exp); P-4; $100K Closing date: 09/08/10

125 REGIONAL OFFICER, Air Traffic Mgmt & Search & Rescue; Int'l Civil Aviation Org (ICAO); (PC 2010/32/P-4); Lima, Peru
(AdvDeg: Aviat-RelatedDiscip/AirTrafficMgmt (ATM); 10 yrs air traffic controller exp); P-4; $97K Closing date: 09/09/10

126 COMPUTER SYSTEMS OFFICER; Econ Commission for LatinAm & Caribbean (ECLAC); (10-IST-ECLAC-15947-R-SANTIAGO); Chile
(AdvDeg: ElectricalEngin/ElectronicEngin/CompSci; 5+ yrs exp; Sp); P-3; $82K Closing date: 09/10/10

127 SENIOR FIELD PROGRAM OFFICER; Food & Agriculture Org (FAO); (2444-RAP); Bangkok, Thailand
(AdvDeg: Agri; 10 yrs dev cntry dev coop prog/proj exp); P-5; $121K Closing date: 09/10/10

128 FISHERY & AQUACULTURE OFFICER; Food & Agriculture Org (FAO); (2446-SLC); Bridgetown, Barbados
(AdvDeg: MarineBiology/FisheriesSci/FisheriesEcon; 7 yrs exp; Fr & Sp); P-4; $104K Closing date: 09/10/10

129 FINANCE OFFICER (Operations); Int'l Maritime Org (IMO); (V.N. 10-13); London, UK
(Deg: Fin; 5+ yrs exp); P-2; $78K Closing date: 09/10/10

130 JUDICIAL AFFAIRS OFFICER/Dept of Peacekp Ops; UN Secretariat (UN); (10-JUR-PMSS-424601-R-MULTIPLE D/S); Multiple D/S
(AdvDeg: Law; 5+ yrs (1+ yr int'l) exp); P-3; $TBD Closing date: 09/10/10

131 CORRECTIONS OFFICER/Dept of Peacekp Ops; UN Secretariat (UN); (10-JUR-PMSS-424597-R-MULTIPLE D/S); Multiple D/S
(AdvDeg: Law/CrimJust/SocSci/Mgmt; 7+ yrs (1+ yrs int'l) exp); P-4; $TBD Closing date: 09/10/10

132 CORRECTIONS OFFICER/Dept of Peacekp Ops; UN Secretariat (UN); (10-JUR-PMSS-424585-R-MULTIPLE D/S); Multiple D/S
(AdvDeg: Law/CrimJust/SocSci/Mgmt; 5+ yrs (1+ yrs int'l) exp); P-3; $TBD Closing date: 09/10/10

133 SENIOR JUDICIAL AFFAIRS OFFICER;   UN Secretariat (UN);   (10-JUR-PMSS-424605-R-MULTIPLE D/S);
Multiple D/S
 (AdvDeg: Law; 10+ yrs (1+ yrs dev cntry) exp);   P-5; $TBD Closing date: 09/10/10

134 JUDICIAL AFFAIRS OFFICER;   UN Secretariat (UN);   (10-JUR-PMSS-424603-R-MULTIPLE D/S);
Multiple D/S
 (AdvDeg: Law; 7+ yrs (1+ yrs dev cntry) exp);   P-4; $TBD Closing date: 09/10/10

135 MAINTENANCE ENGINEER;   Prep Comm for Comprehensive Nucl-Test-Ban Treaty Org (CTBTO); (VA197-38-2010);
Vienna, Austria
 (Deg: ElectricalEngin/SysEngin/Geophysics/NuclSci-Engin; 5+ exp);   P-3; $93K Closing date: 09/11/10

136 ECONOMIC AFFAIRS OFFICER;   UN Econ&SocComm Asia&Pacific (ESCAP); (10-ECO-ESCAP TID TPS-15641-R-
BANGKOK); Thailand
 (AdvDeg: Econ/Int'lTrade; 5+ yrs exp);   P-3; $83K Closing date: 09/11/10

137 SOC AFFAIRS OFCR (Gender Aff Div); Econ Commission for LatinAm & Caribbean (ECLAC); (10-SOC-ECLAC-16010-R-
SANTIAGO); Chile
 (AdvDeg: Sociol/Econ/Law/Anthropol; 7+ yrs exp; Sp);   P-4; $100K Closing date: 09/13/10

138 HEAD, Infrastructure & Facilities Management 2/;   North Atlantic Treaty Org (NATO);   (A 42(2010));   Brussels,
Belgium
 (Deg: CivilEngin/Arch/FacilitiesMgmt; 10+ yrs exp; Fr);   A5; $166K Closing date: 09/13/10

139 SENIOR EXTERNAL RELATIONS & PROJECTS OFFICER; UN Relief & Works Agency (UNRWA);   (10-HQ-JR-61);
Jerusalem
 (AdvDeg: PolSci/Int'lRel/PblcAdm/Law/Econ; 8+ yrs nat'l-int'l org & 3+ yrs sr lvl exp; Fr);   P-4; $105K Closing date:
09/13/10

140 HEAD, Subreg Ofc for N&CentrlSW Asia; UN Econ&SocComm Asia&Pacific ; (10-ADM-ESCAP SANCA-16018-R-ALMATA)(G));
Kazakhstn
 (AdvDeg: Econ/SocSci; 10+ yrs (incl int'l) exp; Rus);   P-5; $127K Closing date: 09/14/10

141 ECONOMIST;   Food & Agriculture Org (FAO);   (CP/TCI-021);   Rome, Italy
 (AdvDeg: Econ/Agri-FoodEcon/AgriBus; 7 yrs exp; Fr/Arabic/Rus);   P-4; $110K Closing date: 09/15/10

142 SERVICE CENTER MANAGER;   UN Development Prog (UNDP);   (18067) Kinshasa, Dem Rep of Congo
 (AdvDeg: Bus-PblcAdmin/Fin/Econ; 10 yrs nat'l-int'l exp; Fr);   P-5; $133K Closing date: 09/15/10

143 FINANCE OFFICER – Accounts;   Prep Comm for Comprehensive Nucl-Test-Ban Treaty Org (CTBTO); (VA151-41-2010);
Vienna, Austria
 (AdvDeg: Fin/BusAdm; 7+ yrs (2+ yrs int'l) exp);   P-4; $111K Closing date: 09/17/10

144 COMMUNICATION & WEB ADMINISTRATOR; Int'l Cntr for Stdy of Preservatn & Restoratn of Cultural Prop (ICCROM);
(N/A); Rome, Italy
 (AdvDeg: IT/CompGraphics/Archaeol/Architect/UrbanPlan/Heritage-MuseumStdys/ArtHist; relevnt exp; P-3; $91K Closing date:
09/17/10

145 CHIEF, Procurement Section;   Prep Comm for Comprehensive Nucl-Test-Ban Treaty Org (CTBTO); (VA165-40-2010);
Vienna, Austria
 (AdvDeg: Pblc-BusAdm/Law; 10+ yrs (4+ yrs int'l & extnsv adm) exp);   P-5; $135K Closing date: 09/18/10

146 NETWORK TEAM LEADER;   Int'l Atomic Energy Agency (IAEA);   (2010/084);   Vienna,
Austria
 (Deg: CompSci/Engin/InfoSysSecCert; 7+ yrs LAN/WAN engineer exp);   P-4; $111K Closing date: 09/20/10

147 SECTION HEAD, Nucl Pwr Technology Dev Section;   Int'l Atomic Energy Agency (IAEA);   (2010/087);   Vienna,
Austria
 (AdvDeg: Nucl-EnginDiscip; 10 yrs (3 yrs int'l) exp);   P-5; $135K Closing date: 09/20/10

148 KNOWLEDGE MANAGEMENT ANALYST;   Int'l Atomic Energy Agency (IAEA);   (2010/078);   Vienna,
Austria
 (AdvDeg: Mgmt/HRM/Int'lStdys; 2+ (incl int'l) exp);   P-2; $77K Closing date: 09/20/10

149 TEAM LEADER (Water Reactor Technology Development); Int'l Atomic Energy Agency (IAEA);   (2010/089);   Vienna,
Austria
 (AdvDeg: Nucl-Mechanical-ChemEngin; 10+ yrs (incl int'l) exp);   P-5; $135K Closing date: 09/20/10

150 PROGRAM OFFICER;   UN Environment Program (UNEP); (10-ADM-UN ENVIRONMENT PROGRAM-15277-R-GENEVA
(O));   Switz
 (AdvDeg: Econ/EnvirEcon; 7+ yrs exp);   P-4; $130K Closing date: 09/21/10

151 SPECIAL ASSISTANT to the Director; UN Environment Prog (UNEP); (10-ADM-UN ENVIRONMENT PROGRAM-15873-R-
PARIS); France
 (AdvDeg: EnvirSci/Mgmt/PolSci/Law; 5+ yrs nat'l-int'l exp; Fr);   P-3; $94K Closing date: 09/24/10

153 TRANSPORT OFFICER/Dept of Peacekp Ops;   UN Secretariat (UN); (10-LOG-PMSS-424657-R-MULTIPLE D/S);

Multiple D/S
   (AdvDeg: MechanicalEngin/Trnsprt/Logis/Adm/Mgmt; 5+ yrs motor vehicle trnsprt ops mgmt exp);   P-3; $TBD Closing date:
09/26/10

154 TRANSPORT OFFICER/Dept of Peacekp Ops;   UN Secretariat (UN); (10-LOG-PMSS-424659-R-MULTIPLE D/S);
Multiple D/S
   (AdvDeg: MechanicalEngin/Trnsprt/Logis/Adm/Mgmt; 7+ yrs motor vehicle trnsprt ops mgmt exp);   P-4; $TBD Closing date:
09/26/10

152 CHIEF TRANSPORT OFFICER/Dept of Peacekp Ops;   UN Secretariat (UN); (10-LOG-PMSS-424661-R-MULTIPLE D/S);
Multiple D/S
   (AdvDeg: MechanicalEngin/Trnsprt/Logis/Adm/Mgmt; 10+ yrs motor vehicle trnsprt ops mgmt exp);   P-5; $TBD Closing date:
09/26/10

155 SR PROGRAM OFFICER;   UN Environment Prog (UNEP); (10-PGM-UN ENVIRONMENT PROGRAM-15407-R-MEXICO
CITY); Mexico
   (AdvDeg: EnvirPolicy-Sci/NatRsrcesMgmt/DevPlanning; 10+ yrs exp);   P-5; $118K Closing date: 09/27/10

156 ADMINISTRATIVE OFFICER;   UN Environment Prog (UNEP); (10-ADM-UN ENVIRONMENT PROGRAM-15428-R-
NAIROBI(O)); Kenya
   (AdvDeg: BusAdm-Mgmt; 7+ yrs exp);   P-4; $96K Closing date: 09/27/10

157 CHIEF, Urban Govrnance; UN Human Settlmnts Prog (UN-HABITAT); (10-ADM-UN HUMAN SETTLMNTS PROG-15432-R-
NAIROBI); Kenya
   (AdvDeg: Urban-RegionalPlanning/UrbanMgmt-Econ/Arch/Sociol; 10 yrs (5+ yrs int'l coop) exp);   P-5; $116K Closing date:
09/27/10

160 PUBLIC INFORMATION OFFICER/Dept of Peacekp Ops; UN Secretariat (UN);   (10-PUB-PMSS-424673-R-MULTIPLE D/S);
Multiple D/S
   (AdvDeg: StratCommun/Commun/PblcRel/Int'lRel/Broadcastng/BusAdm/Mgmt; 5+ yrs exp; Fr);   P-3; $TBD Closing date:
09/27/10

159 PUBLIC INFORMATION OFFICER/Dept of Peacekp Ops; UN Secretariat (UN);   (10-PUB-PMSS-424675-R-MULTIPLE D/S);
Multiple D/S
   (AdvDeg: StratCommun/Commun/PblcRel/Int'lRel/Broadcastng/BusAdm/Mgmt; 7+ yrs exp; Fr);   P-4; $TBD Closing date:
09/27/10

158 SR PUBLIC INFORMATION OFFICER/Dept of Peacekp Ops; UN Secretariat (UN); (10-PUB-PMSS-424683-R-MULTIPLE
D/S); Multiple D/S
   (AdvDeg: StratCommun/Commun/PblcRel/Int'lRel/Broadcastng/BusAdm/Mgmt; 10+ yrs exp; Fr);   P-5; $TBD Closing date:
09/27/10

162 SPOKESPERSON/Dept of Peacekp Ops;   UN Secretariat (UN); (10-PUB-PMSS-424679-R-MULTIPLE D/S);
Multiple D/S
   (AdvDeg: Commun/Journ/PblcRel; 7+ yrs (incl int'l) exp; Fr);   P-4; $TBD Closing date: 09/27/10

161 SPOKESPERSON/Dept of Peacekp Ops;   UN Secretariat (UN); (10-PUB-PMSS-424681-R-MULTIPLE D/S);
Multiple D/S
   (AdvDeg: StratCommun/Commun/PblcRel/Int'lRel/Broadcastng/BusAdm/Mgmt; 10+ yrs exp; Fr);   P-5; $TBD Closing date:
09/27/10

163 RADIOCOMMUNICATION ENGINEER;   Int'l Telecomm Union (ITU);   (P38-2010);   Geneva,
Switz
   (Deg: TelecomEngin/Sci/Engin/Electrical-ElectronicEngin/Radiocommun; 3+ yrs nat'l-int'l exp; UN lang); P-2; $89K Closing date:
09/29/10

164 PROGRAM OFFICER;   Food & Agriculture Organization (FAO);   (2450-TCS);   Rome, Italy
   (AdvDeg: Econ/Int'lDev; 7 yrs int'l exp; Fr/Sp);   P-4; $110K Closing date: 09/30/10

165 HEAD, Department of Applied Research;   NATO Research Center (NURC);   (7/2010);   La Spezia, Italy
   (Deg: Maritime-Marine-Mechanical-NavalEngin/Acoustics/Oceanog/Physics/OpsRsrch; 6 yrs exp);   A.5; $TBD Closing date:
09/30/10

166 HEAD, Department of Systems Technology;   NATO Research Center (NURC);   (8/2010);   La Spezia, Italy
   (Deg: Maritime-Marine-Mechanical-NavalEngin/Acoustics/Oceanog/Physics/OpsRsrch; 6 yrs exp);   A.5; $TBD Closing date:
09/30/10

167 EXTERNAL RELATIONS OFFICER; UN Econ&SocComm Asia&Pacific (ESCAP);   (10-ADM-ESCAP OES-15937-R-
BANGKOK); Thailand
   (AdvDeg: PblcRel/Int'lRel&Dev/SocSci; 7+ yrs exp; UN lang);   P-4; $100K Closing date: 10/01/10

168 SR INVESTMENT OFCR, Subreg Ofc for Central & Eastern EUR; Food & Agriculture Organization (FAO); (2452-SEU);
Budapest, Hungary
   (AdvDeg: Econ/AgriEcon; 10 yrs exp);   P-5; $118K Closing date: 10/02/10

169 PROGRAM OFFICER;   UN Environment Program (UNEP); (10-ADM-UN ENVIRONMENT PROGRAM-15890-R-
NAIROBI (O)); Kenya
   (AdvDeg: Engin/Geology/Physics/BusAdm; 7+ yrs exp);   P-4; $96K Closing date: 10/02/10

Opportunities for Entry-Level International Professional positions with the UN High Commissioner for Refugees (UNHCR) and the International Organization for Migration (IOM)

The Department of State's Bureau of Population, Refugees, and Migration (PRM) sponsors qualified U.S. citizens for employment in the United Nations High Commissioner for Refugees (UNHCR) Junior Professional Officer (JPO) program and in the International Organization for Migration (IOM) Associate Expert (AE) program. Although the qualifications for JPO and AE positions vary by assignment, generally speaking, a graduate or law degree in a relevant discipline and proficiency in at least one U.N. working language in addition to English are preferred.

Competitive applicants generally possess three (3) or more years of work experience in a developing country and an academic background in fields related to human rights, forced migration, humanitarian assistance, development or immigration law, for example. Prior work experience in or familiarity with the UN system or IOM is also helpful. PRM-sponsored JPOs and AEs serve as entry-level international professional officers (the UN P-2 level) for 2 or 3 years in many countries throughout the world. For additional information regarding the program, including any current vacancies and how to apply go to http://www.state.gov/g/prm/c25774.htm or visit PRM's website at www.state.gov/g/prm and follow the link under "What We Do." Applicants should be aware that the process is very competitive and that successful candidates are expected to deploy within approximately 2 months of being selected.

FOOTNOTES:

1/ Salaries are NET (after taxes) and include a cost-of-living/post adjustment that can fluctuate. Minimum salaries are quoted (for persons with

   dependents); higher salaries may be negotiated. Salary data is from actual vacancy announcements or other UN sources and subject to change.

2/ For NATO Applicants ONLY: Please send a copy of the NATO application and any questions about the position to USNATOPERSONNEL@state.gov (6/9)

N.B: 1. We are unable to include on this list all the OPEN UN Department of Peacekeeping Operations (DPKO) positions that appear on the UN's website. If interested in viewing these positions, please check the following site: UN Secretariat (UN)   (https//jobs.un.org)

2. Multiple D/S = Multiple Duty Stations

3. UN Languages: English, French, Spanish, Arabic, Chinese, and Russian

CONTACT INFORMATION
(For U.S. Citizens Only)
UN Employment Information & Assistance Unit
U.S. Department of State
2201 C Street, N.W., Room 4808
Washington, D.C. 20520
EmploymentUN@state.gov

http://www.state.gov/p/io/empl/

Every effort is made to provide accurate and relevant information in this vacancy listing. However, we cannot guarantee that the information contained in this list is in all cases complete and free of error. Each job seeker/interested party should confirm the information listed here with the organization in question. The U.S. Government and the U.S. State Department assume no liability for the accuracy, completeness, or usefulness of any information or process disclosed herein.

www.ingramcontent.com/pod-product-compliance
Lightning Source LLC
Chambersburg PA
CBHW022109170526
45157CB00004B/1551